*the*
# POWER
*of your*
# PATRIARCHAL
# BLESSING

# Other Books By Gayla Wise

The Sign of the Son of Man: The Shechinah
Value-able Ideas for Personal Progress
Help for Gospel Lessons
I Am a Latter-day Saint (Mormon)

# *the* POWER *of your* PATRIARCHAL BLESSING

BY

## GAYLA WISE

spring creek
**BOOK COMPANY**

Provo, Utah

ISBN 978-1-932898-75-0
e. 1

Published by:
Spring Creek Book Company
P.O. Box 50355
Provo, Utah 84605-0355

www.springcreekbooks.com

Cover design © Spring Creek Book Company

Printed in the United States of America
10 9 8 7 6 5 4 3 2 1
Printed on acid-free paper

Library of Congress Cataloging-in-Publication Data
Wise, Gayla.
  The power of your patriarchal blessing / by Gayla Wise.
      p. cm.
  Includes index.
  ISBN 978-1-932898-75-0 (pbk. : alk. paper)
  1. Patriarchal blessings (Mormon Church) I. Title.

BX8643.P36W57 2007
289.3'32--dc22
                                    2007032809

# ACKNOWLEDGMENT

A huge thank you goes to all who shared their insights, stories, and experiences. Your comments reinforced my belief that this book is important. I also acknowledge the hand of God in finding you.

Any additions for future printings, especially by those whose lineage is from one of the so-called "lost" tribes, is welcome and encouraged.

Send your comments to the author in care of Spring Creek Books at **public_relations@springcreekbooks.com.**

# FOREWORD

## by Darla Isackson

I've heard that the veil is not to keep us from remembering God—somehow we always feel His reality. Instead, it is to keep us from remembering who we are, because if we knew, life would be no test. Every person I know well is on a quest to understand better who he or she really is. Since we can't remember, we yearn for clues. Patriarchal blessings give us some of the most important and trustworthy insights to personal reality that we will ever receive.

The quest is becoming more urgent. People are struggling harder to feel their identity and their meaning. In these winding-up scenes of the last days, knowing who we are in the Lord's view can be the anchor to hold us steady in life's stormy seas, the shield to keep us safe from Satan's deceptions.

I think every attack from Satan on me personally has been an attack on my identity. Every way he has tried to discourage me has had something to do with self-doubt—with temptations not to believe in myself or my potential. That is telling. Patriarchal blessings help us see the truth about ourselves. Any book that can help us to learn who we are and to believe in the purposes and promises in our blessings would have to be one of the most important we could read. This inspired book, *The Power of Your Patriarchal Blessing*, is the best I've ever seen to help us do these things.

The author, Gayla Wise, found and interviewed people from numerous tribes. This is one of the most unusual, interesting, and intriguing things I've heard of in a long time. Her research, including fascinating insights in regard to the tribes and the blessings promised each one, has important ramifications for all of us. The idea that members of the lost tribes are being found through patriarchal blessings is stunning to me.

I believe the outstanding benefit of reading this book is that it can lead to important personal revelations. It has for me. The best moments of my life have been when I have had glimpses of my spirit self or of the real spirit identity of my husband or children. This uplift keeps me going and helps me believe in our true worth and how much we all have to look forward to. Since these revelations have so often come while studying our patriarchal blessings, I believe this book can be an incredible tool. Because Gayla Wise shows us how to use the power of our blessings, this book will likely help every reader have more of those heavenly glimpses.

Darla Isackson,
author and editor

# Table of Contents

# TO THE READER

Since I struggled to understand my patriarchal blessing, I suspected others did too. So I began asking people how they had used or come to understand their blessings. I hoped that by gathering insights into a book I could come to understand and use my own blessing and that the result would bless us all.

Unlike most books, each chapter is free-standing. You do not have to read from beginning to end. You can read what meets your needs today and come back and read another place tomorrow.

I have respected the private nature of blessings. Quotes are not given from people's blessings except those published first in the *Ensign* or other sources. People who have shared stories or insights about their blessings are identified by coded initials rather than by name. All the stories are true.

Through this book I hope you will come to value, appreciate, understand, and use your blessing. After many years in the search, I stand in awe of patriarchal blessings—and of who you really are.

Gayla Wise

# CHAPTER 1

## Your Sacred Friend

Would you like a best friend who sees great worth in you and encourages you to become your best? Maybe you would like one who makes you feel better when you are down, or one who is there for you at any time. Your patriarchal blessing can be this best friend. But if you don't know how to understand it or how to use it in your life, your blessing may be a giant puzzle with missing pieces. Whether you have yet to receive your blessing, or it lies buried under clutter in a drawer, you can turn your sacred patriarchal blessing into a best friend.

Meeting a new friend is easier if someone introduces you and tells you a little about him. Similarly, getting acquainted with patriarchal blessings in general can help you feel more comfortable with your own. Then, the more time you spend together and the more experiences you share, the more you will come to know and appreciate your sacred blessing-friend.

What exactly is a patriarchal blessing? When we meet earthly friends, we find out about them by asking questions, so let's ask a couple. What are patriarchal blessings for? or, why do we have them?

The answer is rooted in the doctrine that says, "I am a child of God. He knows me personally and loves me." An equally important doctrine teaches that the heavens are open, and direct revelation from God is possible. A third truth is also evident—when we came to this earth, we brought talents and assignments with us. When these beliefs are combined, the logical conclusion is that God can directly reveal information to, for, and about us for guidance in our lives.

Of course such guidance can come in numerous ways—answers to prayers, for example—but to allow us to see ourselves as God himself sees us, He offers His personal blessing to each one of us individually. This divine perspective of ourselves is one of the great purposes of a patriarchal blessing. Indeed, this perspective is in itself one of the greatest blessings given.

To understand the importance of such perspective, realize that our self-image influences how we act. For instance, if we think we can't do an assignment, we can fail by failing to begin. Lack of belief in ourselves translates into lack of success. But if our blessing tells us we will do things we thought we couldn't do, then the equation changes. Now we believe that somehow we will be able to do the assignment. The blessing has changed our self-concept, our behavior, and our success rate.

As we begin to see God's view of us, we can use our blessings to help us become what He wants us to become. Our blessings, then, are intended to help us achieve our potential. One patriarch related that while he was a missionary, his mission president told him "a patriarchal blessing was an insight into what we had been in the pre-existence and what it was our privilege to become here. [When I reread it], it took on a new meaning of importance."[1]

Joseph Fielding Smith wrote, "The main purpose of the blessing is to be a guide to the individual who receives it, to encourage him, to direct him, to help him as he journeys through life." He added, "I think you will find [it] a great comfort, a guide, and a protection to you."[2]

An American prisoner of World War II had suffered greatly for three years. In telling his story, he wrote:

> *Finally, I had had enough and decided to give up. I had seen others give up. It was invariably fatal.... One day [I refused to] work any longer.... [The guard] beat me, and afterwards, as I lay in my bed waiting for the end to come, I took out ... my patriarchal blessing.*

*As I read my blessing, I thought of my grandfather, the patriarch who had given me the blessing, and my dear mother, who had patiently taken down every word. The words softened me. Maybe ... there was a future for me after all.* [3]

For him, the comfort, guidance, and protection the blessing provided was immediate. He continued, "That day my spirits were lifted, and I determined that I would hang on. I had beaten my enemy." [4] Within a short time, he was rescued. In those critical moments the blessing saved his life.

In real ways, we, too, can use our blessings to guide and protect us, whether physically or spiritually. We cannot underestimate the power of our blessings to comfort and guide us. As with the prisoner, they can literally or symbolically save our physical or spiritual lives.

In addition, a patriarchal blessing will declare our lineage. This includes the responsibilities and blessings that go with our heritage. When we know we belong to the house of Israel, we also know we have a specific place in an eternal family.

Understanding the purposes of a patriarchal blessing helps us see it as a gift from our Heavenly Father. Many people call it a "letter from home." We can trust Him to give a good gift, a blessing we can treasure. Elaine L. Jack said,

*Think of this—what does a patriarchal blessing say? Have you ever heard of one which says, "I am sorry—you're a loser. Do the best you can on earth, and we'll see you in about seventy years." Of course not! And you never will, because of the divine qualities each of God's children has inherited. A patriarchal blessing is like a road map, a guide, directing you in your walk through life. It identifies your talents and the good things that can be yours.* [5]

Nevertheless, many people feel inadequate to get a blessing. Sometimes they needlessly put off getting it. A young man leaving on his mission shared:

*My patriarchal blessing took a leap of faith for me. I was concerned about my worthiness. I thought, maybe if I wait a little longer I'll get a better one. However, I felt lost at the age of eighteen. Lost in the sense that I did not know what the Lord*

*had in store for me. I thought maybe the Lord would chastise
me. Boy, was I wrong! (F.L.G.)*

Making that leap of faith comes in different ways for different
people. A married woman who loves doing genealogy received her
patriarchal blessing three years ago. She said:

> *At the time I didn't have a testimony of a blessing.*
>
> *While I was listening to the patriarch give me my blessing,
> I was amazed at how he knew my love for genealogy because
> he referred back to genealogy four times and stressed the
> importance of it. After I was done my husband and I were
> walking to the car and I said, "Isn't that strange that he knew
> that I love to do genealogy? How did he know?"*
>
> *My husband said, "that wasn't a blessing from him, that
> was a blessing from the Lord." I felt the Spirit come over me
> so strong that I had tears in my eyes. I have a testimony that
> our patriarchal blessings are really blessings from the Lord.
> (V.M.A.)*

Sometimes our concerns about getting a patriarchal blessing
stem from serious problems. An unwed teenage mother gave up her
baby for adoption. Many months later, she wanted to receive her
patriarchal blessing. She wrote:

> *All the trials, errors, sufferings and repentance allowed me
> to develop my testimony. I had truly come to know my Savior,
> Jesus Christ.... I didn't know the patriarch, but when I met
> him I had a warm feeling.... He excused himself to go into
> another room for personal prayer. When he came back out, he
> was crying. He looked into my eyes and told me that my Lord
> wanted me to know that He has forgiven me. This patriarch
> knew nothing of what I had gone through. Then as he laid his
> hands upon my head, I could feel that there was more than one
> set of hands. (C.N.)*

A convert brother said, "Having been raised most of my earthly
existence without a father, I treasure anything and everything that
brings me closer to my Heavenly Father.... I will never lose the joy
this paper brings to me. Because I know that my Father in Heaven

loves me—and you can know that too.... For anyone that has doubt of who they are or why they are here, I strongly recommend seeking out your own patriarchal blessing!" (V.B.H.)

A young man in seminary shared his personal experience and added a plea.

> When the blessing started, a brilliant warmness filled the room. The room was also filled by a great light. When this happened I felt that there was another personage there helping give my blessing.

> I think it was my brother Matthew. He died at birth of hydrocephalus four or five years before this took place.... All through my patriarchal blessing it felt like my heart would burst of flame....

> I urge you all to have a great wanting to have a patriarchal blessing. I got mine when I was fourteen years old, and it has changed my life. It is a guideline for living. Please get one. It will change your life as it did mine. (K.N.H.)

"Heavenly Father talked to me directly," said one woman. (E.A.) Because the "me" in each experience is different, each experience is different. We should not compare our blessings to those of others or feel they are either less than or more than another's. They are uniquely ours just as each of us is unique. As one woman said, "Your patriarchal blessing does not do me one bit of good." (K.K.#2)

President Gordon B. Hinckley said, "I count my patriarchal blessing as one of the great sacred things of my life.... What a unique, personal, individual, wonderful thing is a patriarchal blessing spoken by authority of the priesthood and the office and calling of patriarch in the name of the Lord Jesus Christ."[6]

Your patriarchal blessing is a personalized, carefully chosen sacred gift from our Heavenly Father. As you become best friends with it, it will guide you back to your heavenly family.

## SOURCES

1. Elmo J. Bergeson, "The Patriarchal Blessing, a Gift and a Guide," *Instructor*, Dec. 1960, p. 420.

2. Joseph Fielding Smith, "Patriarchal Blessings," *Charge to Religious Educators*, Salt Lake City: The Church of Jesus Christ of Latter-day Saints, 1981, pp. 122-123.

3. A. C. Christensen, "Two Pieces of Paper Saved Me," *Ensign*, Feb. 1990, p. 60.

4. *Ibid*, p. 60.

5. Elaine L. Jack, "Identity of a Young Woman," *Ensign*, Nov. 1989, p. 87.

6. Gordon B. Hinckley, "Inspirational Thoughts," *Ensign*, Aug. 1997, p. 5.

# CHAPTER 2

## Answers to Common Questions

What questions do you have about patriarchal blessings? Many commonly asked questions concern preparing for and receiving a blessing. To gain what you need from this chapter, scan through the questions. If you already know the answer to a question, go on to the next one.

*Q.* How do you pronounce the word "patriarchal?"

*A.* Many people mispronounce this word. Webster's dictionary marks it this way: pa-tre-`ar-kel.[1] Be careful not to call it pa-tre-art-i-cal.

*Q.* How old should I be before I receive my blessing?

*A.* There is no set age. The recipient should be worthy and want the blessing and be old enough to appreciate its serious nature. This is loosely interpreted to mean age twelve or older. A former Patriarch to the Church, Eldred G. Smith, stated, "I think the best age is between fifteen and twenty-five."[2] But the blessing may be given at any age.

A ten-year-old boy in a family with sporadic activity "kept bugging" his bishop. He wanted his patriarchal blessing. Finally the bishop sat him down and asked him questions. He gave all the right answers. He knew why he wanted it—it would guide his life. During his teen years he was not very active and would not have sought his blessing. By the time his friends were going on missions, he got it out and read it. It said he would go on a mission, so he got ready and went. Ten was the right age for him to get this blessing. His spirit knew he needed it. Now in his early thirties he is serving in a bishopric. (S.N.#1)

One of the youngest recipients was undoubtedly President Heber J. Grant whose mother took him to the patriarch when he was a baby. Later, as a parent, when his second baby was critically ill, President Grant sent for a friend to assist him in blessing her. Afterward, the two agreed that the child would die without intervention by the Lord. Then the friend, who was a patriarch, said "'Well, the Lord is going to hear.... Go and get a table and a piece of paper, and sit down by the bed; I want to give this baby its patriarchal blessing.'"[3]

Today, since members normally receive only one blessing in a lifetime, we understand why recipients should "be old enough to understand the meaning and purpose and value of a patriarchal blessing."[4]

One Apostle, Elder LeGrand Richards, was eight years old when he received his. For him, it was a special occasion to remember—he and his two brothers were the first to receive blessings under the hands of a newly-called patriarch, his father.

President Spencer W. Kimball received his at age nine. He believed it contributed to his early love for the Lamanite people.

Joseph F. Smith, a Patriarch to the Church, shared this story in General Conference in 1944.

*I think one of the biggest thrills that I have had was a few weeks ago. One day on my appointment sheet I read merely "appointment." There was no name. I asked my secretary who that was, and she mumbled something rather inarticulately. At the appointed hour, my little nine-year-old boy came into my office, beaming all over. On his own initiative he had gone to his bishop and the president of the stake and he brought me his recommendation to have his daddy give him a patriarchal blessing.*[5]

Elder Matthew Cowley also received his blessing early in life, but his story contrasts the others because he didn't know he had it. He told of being a missionary in far-away New Zealand. He and his companion were "giving each other the silent treatment," he said, "and all of a sudden I had a vision. I could see myself as a young child in Colorado. There a man had his hands on my head. My father was sitting at a table writing, and I felt that is [sic] a patriarchal blessing. I had never read it in my life. I didn't know what it was." [6]

The vision came to him as the solution to his problems. After his mother sent his patriarchal blessing, he could see why he was in New Zealand on his mission rather than in Hawaii where he had wanted to go. This knowledge changed him and his mission.

Getting the blessing early in life did not help in Elder Cowley's case, but reading it when he needed it did. Often, young people approaching serious decisions feel a desire to obtain their patriarchal blessings. Others, not feeling ready, postpone it until after marriage, making that decision without the guidance a blessing might have provided. Elder Cowley's experience is an example of why General Authorities ask missionaries to receive and take their blessings with them.

The differences in the stories show that age is not the only, nor the determining, factor for getting a blessing. Desire, understanding, and readiness are more important considerations.

*Q.* Am I too old?

*A.* There is no maximum age. One sixty-three-year-old man overcame his feelings of being too old and received his blessing. He went away rejoicing. Another fine brother joined the Church in his seventies and received his blessing the following year.

However, since the blessing is intended to assist us through our lifetimes, we are encouraged not to procrastinate getting them. As James E. Faust said,

*The patriarchal blessing is primarily a guide to the future, not an index to the past. Therefore, it is important that the*

*recipient be young enough that many of the significant events of life are in the future. I recently heard of a person over ninety years of age who received his patriarchal blessing. It would be interesting to read that blessing.*[7]

Yet if we, like the ninety-year-old, have not received our blessings, we are entitled to them. We need not go through the rest of life without them, just because we have gone without so far and think it's too late to do any good. Also, with the perspective of living eternally, there is much of life yet ahead.

*Q.* My grandfather (or other close relative) is a patriarch in another stake. Can he give me my blessing?

*A.* A patriarch can give blessings to his lineal blood descendants, wherever they live, if they have the appropriate recommend. Thus, a grandfather could give you a blessing, but your uncle could not. One middle-age man recalled receiving his blessing from his grandfather. "It required a 250-mile trip and took planning," he said. "It was special. When I read it, I can almost hear his voice." (E.V.)

*Q.* I don't feel comfortable about going to the patriarch because I don't know him. I've put off getting my blessing because of this. What can I do about it?

*A.* Patriarchs take time to talk with you and get to know you before giving a blessing. They are kind and caring men who will help you feel comfortable. Also, since the blessing is given in the patriarch's home, rather than at the church, the homey atmosphere should help you feel at ease. If meeting new people is difficult for you, you could visit with the patriarch ahead of time. Remember, too, that the blessing is not from the patriarch but from your Heavenly Father who knows you well.

*Q.* Our stake is temporarily without a patriarch. How can I get my blessing?

*A.* Members in such stakes may take a recommend signed by their bishop to a patriarch in a nearby stake.[8]

*Q.* I live in the mission field where we do not have a patriarch. How can I get my blessing?

*A.* Take a recommend from your branch president to a patriarch in a stake where you are able to travel.[9]

*Q.* I left for the military without getting my blessing. Now I would like it. Where do I go to get one?

*A.* The procedure is similar. Check with your bishop, branch president, or LDS chaplain for details.

*Q.* What is required to be ready to receive a blessing?

*A.* One patriarch answered simply, "Above all, faith in the Lord Jesus Christ."[10]

Putting our faith into action helps, too. Others encouraged one fourteen-year-old young man to get his blessing. He reported, "Up to this point I had done nothing that concerned prayer or reading the scriptures. I did both and decided to receive my patriarchal blessing."[11]

*Q.* Others around me are getting their blessings. How can I tell if I'm ready to get mine?

*A.* As a fifteen-year-old girl said, "You need to have the desire yourself."[12] A young man who prepared himself and received his blessing advised, "Don't let friends or family members pressure you into it, but ... make your decision based on what you feel is right."[13]

An individual should not seek a blessing because others in a group are getting one or to satisfy family encouragement. Neither should teachers in Church organizations suggest that "everyone" go get one. To help ensure proper reasons and readiness, all phases of receiving a blessing are the responsibility of the recipient. In addition to having a personal desire, you should feel you understand the value and purpose of a patriarchal blessing.

If you want one but feel hesitant, talk to your parents or your bishop. If you are afraid of what the Lord will expect of you, realize that you have already made commitments to Him when you were baptized. Expectations in your blessing "will not be greatly different." [14] Besides, His expectations of you are the same whether or not you receive the blessing to guide you in fulfilling them.

Do not feel alone if you feel torn between wanting one and not wanting one yet. One Young Women leader said that she hadn't felt ready at sixteen. "I fasted and prayed and got confirmation that I wasn't ready," she said. (T.D.)

*Q*. Who determines readiness?

*A*. The individual first, and ultimately the bishop. Realize, however, that feeling "unready" may cover different excuses that hold us back but may not be valid. An *Ensign* article stated, "You may feel that you are unimportant, too old, and that the Lord has no blessing for you. Or perhaps you have sinned and even though you have repented consider yourself unworthy of a blessing or to receive a blessing. If that is so, I suggest that you make an appointment with your bishop, seek his advice, follow his counsel, and actively and humbly solicit the blessings of heaven." [15]

*Q*. If I get my blessing when I'm not spiritually prepared, does that affect the blessing?

*A*. Patriarchs say it's much harder to give a blessing to someone who is not spiritually prepared. It leaves the patriarch to struggle to give the blessing in spite of the void. Some felt uncertain whether the blessing was as complete as it might otherwise have been. Perhaps it was, perhaps not. If not, then possibly the person could find the meaning later on that the Lord intended.

Prevention of this is best. That's why patriarchs chat with the recipient before giving a blessing. The Spirit tells them things in those few minutes. If the patriarch feels impressed to wait so the recipient can be better prepared, he will say so. However, the responsibility rests on the person receiving the blessing to be as prepared as possible.

*Q*. Am I the only one who wants a blessing but feels hesitant?

*A*. President Hinckley's daughter Virginia H. Pearce told of a typical "reluctance" as the day for getting her blessing approached.

> My anxiety was all about my future. I had heard story after story of remarkable blessings with unusual promises.... What if I didn't have anything in my future? Better not to know. Maybe ... the blessing would only be one or two sentences long....

But her experience was far different from her fears.

> As he placed his hands on my head, there was a steadiness that vaporized all uncertainty. I remember the surprise and wonder of that day, but also of every other time I have read that blessing—the startling news: He knows me. Heavenly Father knows me! And he has a plan for my future.[16]

Bishops report that it is common for young people to receive two or even three recommends before they follow through and receive their blessings. An entire year passed from the time one priest got his first recommend until he actually obtained his blessing. For him it was a year of contemplation and preparation, and although he had wanted it all along, when he received his blessing, he felt the time was right. (L.C.A.)

*Q*. Why do I need a recommend, and how do I get one?

*A*. Because of the sacredness of a blessing, a person should be worthy to receive it. The recommend, a small certificate from the bishop, tells the patriarch you are worthy (not perfect but striving to do what's right) and gives him permission to bless you. To get a recommend, contact your ward executive secretary and make an appointment with your bishop.

*Q*. What will the bishop's recommend interview be like?

*A*. There are no specific questions. One bishop said that the interview is similar to a yearly interview for youth or to priesthood ordination interviews for men and young men. The bishop will visit with you to see that you are worthy and ready. He can also answer questions to help prepare you.

If you find the idea of a bishop's interview intimidating, just remember it can help you grow spiritually. Some people get "hung up" on this step and let it keep them from getting their blessings. Instead, if you want a blessing but are uneasy about getting a recommend, chat informally with your bishop. Let him know you are interested in a blessing and see what he says. Think how good you will feel with a crisp, white recommend in your hand—with your name on it.

*Q.* What if I get in the bishop's office and decide I'm not ready?

*A.* Think of the interview as an opportunity. It will allow you to look at yourself and perhaps do a little soul-searching. An interview is not a pass-fail, now-or-never situation. It's quite all right to talk with the bishop and decide you want to wait.

*Q.* What if I get in the bishop's office and he decides I'm not ready?

*A.* If this happens, you will probably agree with him and feel satisfied about waiting. One bishop asked a woman to wait and to receive her blessing later. He felt that for her own good, "now" was not the right time for her. Their visit became a positive step in her preparation.

*Q.* What's the next step after getting a bishop's recommend?

*A.* Call the stake patriarch and set an appointment. You do not need an interview or signature from the stake presidency.

*Q.* How soon after joining the Church can new members get their blessings?

*A.* Currently, no set timeframe is recommended. The convert should understand the gospel and prepare like anyone else.

A woman who joined the Church in 1975 shared her experience on this question. After baptism, she and her husband were excited and enthusiastic.

*[We started] reading everything we could get our hands on to learn more about the Church. We learned about patriarchal blessings and talked to our bishop about it. We wanted to*

*know what we had to do to get one as we wanted to do all that we should to be valiant servants of the Lord and felt that a patriarchal blessing would help us to do that....*

*The day for our blessing arrived. We were excited and had prepared for it by fasting. The patriarch took our recommends. He stood looking at them for a long time, saying nothing. After what seemed to be forever, he said that he felt a little uncomfortable giving us our blessings as we had only been members of the Church for a few months and that he would feel better if we waited a little longer. We must have looked devastated because he quickly added that perhaps we should have a prayer and then decide what to do.*

*We went into a small room and knelt down for a prayer. He asked my husband to offer it. As we stood up from the prayer he said, "It's all right. We can go ahead." (L.P.)*

*Q.* How do I prepare to receive a blessing?

*A.* One patriarch counseled, "the person receiving the blessing should be humble and prayerful and approach this appointment with the same spirit as though he were going to the temple." [17]

A young woman recommended, "When your time comes, fast and pray for the Spirit to be with you. Pray for your patriarch that he might feel of the Spirit so he will be able to say those things which your Father in Heaven has need for you to know. If you do, your experience will be one you will never forget." [18]

*Q.* Do I need to come fasting?

*A.* Church policy no longer requires you to come fasting, but you are invited to fast. Patriarchs usually recommend it. "It helps the patriarch," one explained. Fasting invites the Spirit. Since the patriarch gives many blessings, it is not practical for him to fast for each one. Therefore, if fasting is used, you are the one to do so.

*Q.* How should I dress?

*A.* Dressing properly is part of preparing to invite the Spirit. Dress so that the Spirit is comfortable coming to bless you. This means dressing as though you were going to church. Patriarchs emphasize that this does help and is important.

*Q.* Who can I bring with me?

*A.* Young people living at home are encouraged to bring their parents. It is better to leave the rest of the family at home, regardless of whether or not they have received their blessings. This needs to be an intimate and sacred time with the Spirit. Including a boyfriend or girlfriend, even a fiancé, is not a good idea. Some couples who did not follow this advice later wished they had.

This counsel has developed through wisdom by experience over the years. In the early history of the church "patriarchal blessing meetings" were often held. This concept helps us understand the protection of privacy with today's guidelines.

*Q.* Can I bring my parents if they are nonmembers?

*A.* If you are a young person living with nonmember parents, invite them to come with you. They may choose to do so. Patriarchs report that not only does the Spirit come, but that nonmember parents feel it. They experience this as a time of rejoicing with a son or daughter whom they love.

*Q.* What does a patriarch do?

*A.* The patriarch serves as a mouth for the Lord. His calling requires him to be humble and in tune with the Spirit so he can hear the message the Lord wants to give you.

*Q.* How does a patriarch know what to say?

*A.* A patriarch will tell experiences to answer this question, illustrating that of himself he does not know what to say. The concepts in the blessing come directly from the Lord. The vocabulary and sentence structure may be the patriarch's. Then again, they may be the Lord's, or from scripture, or on occasion even words that the recipient recognizes from his own life such as phrases from his own prayers.

*Q.* How does the patriarch know the lineage?

*A.* The lineage comes through inspiration. One patriarch who knew he would be giving a blessing to an Oriental brother was so concerned about the lineage that he prayed fervently. The answer that came was, to him, intellectually impossible. Because of this, he struggled, pleading in prayer, "Please, inspire me right." Again he received the impossible answer. When he put his hands on the brother, he received the same answer—Ephraim. There was no doubt in his mind that it was the right tribe, regardless of what he thought personally. Incidentally, his own Oriental daughter-in-law was from Manasseh. (H.A.K.)

Our lineage is in our blood, undoubtedly something physical there. As Joseph Fielding Smith said, a patriarch "has the right of inspiration to declare the literal descent of the person receiving the blessing; he does not have authority to assign that individual to any tribe." [19]

*Q.* Why don't my brothers and sisters and I all have the same lineage?

*A.* This situation is actually quite common. Few of us are purebred. This is not much different from a family that has blue-eyed, brown-eyed, and maybe hazel-eyed children.

In General Conference, President James E. Faust explained that the tribes have inter-mixed with one another, and the House of Israel is spread throughout much of humanity. He said, "The blessing of one tribe, therefore, may be dominant in one child, and the blessing of another tribe dominant in yet another child. So, children from the same parents could receive the blessings of different tribes." [20]

As a Patriarch to the Church said, "We are mixtures. Many of us are mixtures of several tribes of Israel and so it is the right of the patriarch to declare that line through which the blessings shall come." [21] The declared lineage, like any genetic trait, is the dominant tribe within us.

*Q.* What is the purpose of the declaration of lineage?

*A.* In short, God's house is a house of order, and our lineage indicates the line through which our blessings come. These include the priesthood and the promises given to Abraham of inheritance and posterity. (See chapter 4 for more detail.) We see pieces of this process with ancient Israel, with ancient America as a land for Ephraim and Manasseh, and with modern Jews (Judah) returning to their promised land.

*Q.* How can I tell if my lineage is by bloodline or by adoption?

*A.* It doesn't matter. The Lord promised Abraham, "And I will bless them through thy name; for as many as receive this Gospel shall be called after thy name, and shall be accounted thy seed, and shall rise up and bless thee, as their father." (Abr. 2:10.) Another verse reads, "And if ye be Christ's, then are ye Abraham's seed and heirs according to the promise." (Gal. 3:29.) Since the Lord said it, we don't need to worry about the question.

In addition Joseph Smith said, "The effect of the Holy Ghost upon a Gentile is to purge out the old blood, and make him actually of the seed of Abraham." [22] Since the blood becomes the same, this explains why, in the end, "adoption" doesn't matter.

*Q.* How is the blessing recorded?

*A.* When the patriarch gives your blessing, he will use a tape recorder. Later he or a secretary, who is called for this purpose and will keep the contents confidential, will transcribe it. Two copies will be made which he will sign. One will be mailed to you. The other copy will be preserved in a record book. When the book is full, the patriarch will forward it to Church offices for permanent record keeping.

*Q.* Why is the blessing recorded in Church archives?

*A.* One obvious reason is as a backup copy for the recipient. Through centralized records, it also becomes available to direct line family members. But these are lesser reasons.

A Patriarch to the Church said there is a "fundamental principle" involved. Once "given and properly recorded, they are just as eternal and binding upon us through our faithfulness as were the blessings which were given by Adam, Abraham, Jacob or any of the former patriarchs in the times which have passed."[23] It is a way of preserving the blessing spiritually as well as physically.

Q. Can I read my parents' blessings and learn about me?

A. Sometimes you can gain insight into yourself in this way. To read your parents' blessings, ask their permission if they are living.

Q. How many patriarchal blessings can I have?

A. Church policy states that every worthy member is entitled to receive a patriarchal blessing. General Authorities advise that one should generally be sufficient in a lifetime. Years ago, many members received more than one, but this practice has been discontinued. However, if the declaration of lineage is somehow omitted, the person should receive not a second blessing but what is called an "addendum."

Q. If I really feel a need for a second blessing, can I get it?

A. Patriarchs advise against it. Joseph F. Smith stated, "wherever there is to be an exception, ... [it] should be made very, very carefully ... after careful and very thorough consideration."[24] This advice stands today.

The bishop has the responsibility to decide. Wanting another one or not understanding the current one generally are not adequate reasons. Uncommon circumstances for needing a second blessing should exist.

One convert's blessing was restricted only to details of a full-time mission and ended with clear indication that this was what the Lord wanted him to know for now. In this rare case, he actually needed a second blessing which he did receive later. (N.A.) Due to unique circumstances, a woman knew that her life span had been extended. She also needed and received

a patriarch's blessing to cover the additional years. (T.I.)
Technically, these were not second blessings but addendums.

Those who obtain an addendum for other reasons often
report that it said "the same thing" as the original blessing. Most
patriarchs will counsel that, rather than requesting another
blessing, concerned members prayerfully work to understand
the one they have.

We are, of course, welcome to seek additional blessings from
someone other than a patriarch. Through the patriarchal order
of the priesthood, it is the right and privilege of the husband
and father to bless his family. Those without this resource can
turn to priesthood leaders for similar blessings.

*Q.* How often should I read my patriarchal blessing?

*A.* One patriarch responded, "How often should you read the
scriptures?" He added, "It's common for your blessing to be more
clear every time you read it." (H.I.) Another said, "Some people
get their blessing and might read it when they get it and then
put it in a drawer. It can't do them any good unless they read it.
Read it at least once a month, maybe more often." (N.E.)

Some people read theirs every fast Sunday so they have
a regular time to remember. One young adult liked to get up
before her roommates on Sundays and use the quiet time to
ponder her blessing. Others designate twice a year such as New
Year's or Easter and their birthday. One brother reduced his to
wallet size so he can carry it with him everywhere he goes.

One woman wasn't sure where her blessing was so hadn't
read it for some time. As a nurse in intensive care, one day she
checked on an agitated patient who waved a paper in her hand.
It was the patient's patriarchal blessing, dated two weeks before
she entered the hospital. The woman was not expected to live,
and the nurse read it aloud thinking it was too late for the
blessings to occur. When she put it back in the patient's hand,
"she clenched it tightly as if it were a life preserver." The woman
unexpectedly improved and "for all I know she may have lived to
see some of the promises [fulfilled]," said the nurse. "I will never

forget what that patient did for me. She impressed me to go home, find and read my own blessing, and cherish it as she did hers. Ever since that time, I have kept my patriarchal blessing next to my bed, where I read it frequently."[25]

Read and ponder with faith. If you reread it often enough to memorize part or all of it, so much the better. The idea is to make it useful. If you remember what it says, you can apply it in your daily life. It seems obvious, but the reason we receive a printed copy is so that we can read it.

*Q.* Who can I show it to?

*A.* The guideline is to keep your blessing sacred. Show it only to immediate family members who will respect its sacredness. A couple of experiences show why. "As a youth I shared some of my blessing with friends. They weren't as impressed with 'who I was' as I was," said one woman. (N.K.#1) A mother "bragged" to a few people about her son's patriarchal blessing. Then "it didn't come out quite like I said. My son was resentful because I shared without his permission." (C.R.#2)

*Q.* Who can I ask to help me understand it?

*A.* Caring parents, grandparents, or a spouse may encourage and counsel with you about your blessing. Some have taken a blessing to their patriarch for insight. However, Elder Boyd K. Packer said we should not "ask others to interpret it. Neither the patriarch nor the bishop can or should interpret it."[26] Ultimately, He who gave the blessing knows its meaning. Ask Him.

*Q.* What is the difference between a patriarchal blessing and fortune telling?

*A.* Sometimes people get confused with the two although they are very different. Virginia H. Pearce said that as a fifteen-year old anticipating her blessing, "I wondered if I would go on a mission—would I marry—would there be children—how many? As you can see, I didn't really understand the difference between a patriarchal blessing and a Chinese fortune cookie.

But I did understand one important difference: I didn't believe in messages in cookies, but I did believe in patriarchal blessings. I was prepared to believe anything that was said, or not said."[27] In short, a patriarchal blessing is true revelation from our Heavenly Father and is reliable.

*Q.* What is the difference between a father's blessing and a patriarchal blessing?

*A.* Robert C. Fletcher, a patriarch, illustrated the difference. He had given a patriarchal blessing followed immediately by a father's blessing to his son preparing to leave on a mission. He recalled, "The contrast was interesting. The patriarchal blessing put his whole life in perspective, identifying his lineage, and giving blessings and admonition to provide guidance and comfort for the rest of his life. The father's blessing pertained primarily to the near future, intended to sustain him over the next two years." [28]

The patriarch added that while both blessings were transcribed, the patriarchal blessing would be preserved at Church headquarters whereas the other would be kept with family records. The first required a recommend while the second did not. He explained that because he was both patriarch and father, he could have combined either blessing into the other but chose to keep them separate.

*Q.* I've lost mine. Can I get another copy?

*A.* To obtain a duplicate copy of your own patriarchal blessing, send a written request to the address below. Include your full name as it appears on the blessing, your date of birth, approximately when your blessing was given, and the name of the patriarch and stake where it was given. As of March 1, 2007, there is no charge. Mail to:

Church History Library

Patriarchal Blessings

50 East North Temple Street

Salt Lake City, UT 84150-3420

Allow 30 days for processing. For a recorded message to update this information, call 1-801-240-3581. If you wish to speak with someone, call 1-801-240-2272.

*Q.* Can I obtain a copy of anyone's patriarchal blessing besides my own?

*A.* You can request your spouse's, a direct descendant's, or a deceased direct-line ancestor's using the information in the previous answer. Supply as much of the requested data as possible. Include your relationship to the person. Requests are limited to four copies. Copies for deceased persons take longer to process.

## SOURCES

1. *Webster's Ninth New Collegiate Dictionary*, Springfield: Merriam-Webster Inc., 1984, p. 863.

2. Eldred G. Smith, *Conference Report*, Apr. 1960, p. 66.

3. Heber J. Grant, *Gospel Standards*, comp. G. Homer Durham, Salt Lake City: *The Improvement Era*, 1943, p. 12.

4. Eldred G. Smith, *Conference Report*, Apr. 1960, p. 66.

5. Joseph F. Smith "The Significance of Patriarchal Blessings," *Improvement Era*, Nov. 1944, p. 720.

6. Matthew Cowley, *Matthew Cowley Speaks*, Salt Lake City: Deseret Book Co., 1954, p. 424.

7. James E. Faust, "Priesthood Blessings," *Ensign*, Nov. 1995, p. 63.

8. See Boyd K. Packer, "The Stake Patriarch," *Ensign*, Nov. 2002, p. 45.

9. *Ibid.*

10. Carl Ringger, "What Are the Requirements in Preparing for a Patriarchal Blessing?" *New Era*, Apr. 1972, p. 11.

11. "Q&A" *New Era*, Mar. 1992, p. 19.

12. "Q&A" *New Era*, Mar. 1992, p. 18.

13. "Q&A" *New Era*, Mar. 1992, p. 19.

14. "Q&A" *New Era*, Mar. 1992, p. 17.

15. Richard D. Allred, "The Lord Blesses His Children through Patriarchal Blessings," *Ensign*, Nov. 1997, p. 27.

16. Virginia H. Pearce, "Faith Is the Answer," *Ensign*, May 1994, pp. 93-94.

17. Elmo J. Bergeson, "The Patriarchal Blessing, a Gift and a Guide," *Instructor*, Dec. 1960, p. 421.

18. "Q&A" *New Era*, Mar. 1992, p. 19.

19. Joseph Fielding Smith, *Doctrines of Salvation*, comp. Bruce R. McConkie, Salt Lake City: Bookcraft, 1956, vol. 3, p. 171.

20. James E. Faust, *Ensign*, "Priesthood Blessings," Nov. 1995, p. 64.

21. Eldred G. Smith, *Conference Report*, Apr. 1960, pp. 65-66.

22. Joseph Fielding Smith, comp., *Teachings of the Prophet Joseph Smith*, Salt Lake City: Deseret Book Co., 1977, p. 150.

23. Hyrum G. Smith, *Conference Report*, Apr. 1924, p. 89.

24. Joseph F. Smith, *Conference Report*, Oct. 1944, p. 112.

25. Paula T. Weed, "Clinging to Faith in Intensive Care," *Ensign*, Sept. 2000, p. 65.

26. Boyd K. Packer, "The Stake Patriarch," *Ensign*, Nov. 2002, p. 43.

27. Virginia H. Pearce, "Faith Is the Answer," *Ensign*, May 1994, p. 93.

28. "Q&A," *New Era*, Jan. 1978, p. 18.

# CHAPTER 3

## The Line of Patriarchs

Long ago Adam became the first patriarch, a hero in a real-life story. The pattern of what he did and said, and of patriarchs after him, helps us understand our patriarchal blessings. You can skip this chapter if you wish, but think of it this way:

Suppose you go to a party and are invited to play a game. You love games and are excited to play. You're next! But wait! Nobody told you the rules. That's what it's like if you get your patriarchal blessing without any idea of where they came from or why we have them or what this background means to you. Looking at early patriarchs helps us understand the eternal nature and significance of our blessings.

## ADAM

The root words of patriarch mean "chief father." The chief father for this earth is Adam, the father of us all. As the first patriarch, he presided over his multi-generational family until his death. Each son likewise became a patriarch to his own progeny. This system provided not only spiritual direction but also political government and was called The Patriarchal Order. This was a system of orderliness patterned after our heavenly home. Love of the father for his family permeated his guidance over them. Through the priesthood, the father could also bless his children, which blessing would be binding through their righteousness. In a true and double sense, then, as Adam blessed his posterity, he gave them patriarchal blessings.

Through revelation we know that three years before his death Adam summoned a large family gathering of those "who were righteous." (D&C 207:53.) Joseph Smith said, "I saw Adam in the valley of Adam-ondi-Ahman. He called together his children and blessed them with a patriarchal blessing." [1] Orson Pratt said the blessing was "the object" of this gathering. [2] Also, Adam "preached ... and pronounced upon them his great and last patriarchal blessing."[3] In it, according to Wilford Woodruff, Adam "prophesied what should take place even till the coming of Messiah, which prophecy is said to be written in the Book of Enoch." [4]

We picture Adam giving his vast family one grand united blessing as their "chief father." As the eldest patriarch, he blessed them and gave them vision for their lives through prophecy. This was a true patriarchal blessing as surely as though he had placed his hands on their heads one by one.

Joseph Smith explained the purpose and eternal importance of Adam's family conference. "This is why Adam blessed his posterity; he wanted to bring them into the presence of God."[5]

# ABRAHAM

Through the generations that followed, the Patriarchal Order of the priesthood and of family government continued the pattern set by Adam. In time, Abraham became a great patriarch with the covenant promise that through him all people would be blessed.

We learn much about blessings by studying the covenants God made with Abraham. We might say God personally gave Abraham his patriarchal blessing because God gave Abraham the promises as a father to his earthly son. God revealed to Abraham the great blessings that would be his through faithfulness. These elements are present in our own blessings. The main difference is that we have an intermediary who speaks the words.

Because patriarchal blessings today sometimes refer to the "blessings of Abraham" or promise the "blessings of Abraham, Isaac and Jacob," we need to understand what these promises entail. Basically the blessings were two-fold with double meaning. God promised Abraham inheritance and posterity. On a limited earthly level this meant a physical land in which to live and a family with which to enjoy it. On the second, higher level, inheritance meant an eternal, celestial estate, and posterity meant an eternally increasing offspring. God offered the blessing; Abraham validated it. Abraham's overwhelming opportunity hinged on his relationship with the Lord who had emphatically declared, "I will ... be a God unto thee." (Gen. 17:7.) Abraham's obedience and faithfulness were crucial to turn the promised blessings into reality.

Our promised blessings, like Abraham's, demand our diligence if we are to claim them. Nevertheless we are promised the blessings of Abraham. First of all, regardless of our origin, our patriarchal blessings tell us we are of the house of Abraham. Then the Lord said, "This promise is yours also, because ye are of Abraham, and the promise was made unto Abraham." (D&C 132:31.)

# ISAAC

Isaac was the long-awaited son promised to Abraham. The establishment of the covenant lineage through his birth was a miracle showing God's fatherly intent to watch over and nurture Abraham's seed. Isaac followed the footsteps of his father in righteous living and thereby received the same promises. "And the LORD appeared unto him, and said ... I will be with thee, and will bless thee; for ... I will perform the oath which I sware unto Abraham thy father; And I will make thy seed to multiply as the stars of the heaven, and will give unto thy seed all these countries; and in thy seed shall all the nations of the earth be blessed." (Gen. 26:2-4.) He was greatly blessed with riches of the earth and his "seed to multiply" began as two sons.

# JACOB

Jacob and Esau were twin sons of Isaac. Although born only minutes apart, Esau was the elder and therefore entitled to the birthright. The birthright son received all the lands and holdings of the father upon the father's death. The heir also became the ruler or patriarch of the family. As a young man, however, Esau did not value his birthright and literally sold it to Jacob for a bowl of stew.

(See Gen. 25:32-34.) Esau again disqualified himself at forty when he married two Hittite women. Such marriages were forbidden because they were outside the covenant and meant that the descendants were denied the covenant blessings. Therefore Esau's action caused Isaac and Rebekah, his parents, great sorrow. (See Gen. 26:34.)

Nevertheless, as Isaac approached death he asked Esau to prepare a special meal and come for a blessing. Rebekah went to Jacob and said, "my son, obey my voice." (Gen. 27:8) Jacob obeyed. So Jacob arrived first and, because Isaac was blind, received the blessing. Through worthiness, the blessing was Jacob's to receive, and he, his mother, and God knew it. As soon as Jacob left, Esau entered wanting his blessing. Isaac trembled and asked whom he had just blessed. "Yea, [and] he shall be blessed," he stated, validating the blessing. (Gen. 27:33.)

From the depths of Esau's loss we see the great worth of the blessing.

"And when Esau heard the words of his father, he cried with a great and exceeding bitter cry, and said unto his father, Bless me, [even] me also, O my father.

"... Hast thou not reserved a blessing for me?

"And Isaac answered and said unto Esau, Behold, I have made him thy lord, and all his brethren have I given to him for servants; and with corn and wine have I sustained him: and what shall I do now unto thee, my son?

"And Esau said unto his father, Hast thou but one blessing, my father? bless me, [even] me also, O my father. And Esau lifted up his voice, and wept." (Gen. 27: 34, 36-38.)

So Isaac found a father's blessing for the son who would not be without one.

But it was Jacob who then obeyed father and mother for whom to marry, while Esau spitefully married another wife outside the covenant. (See Gen. 28:1-9.)

It was Jacob to whom the Lord appeared and said, "I am the LORD God of Abraham thy father, and the God of Isaac: the land whereon thou liest, to thee will I give it, and to thy seed; And thy seed shall be as the dust of the earth, and thou shalt spread abroad ... and in thee and in thy seed shall all the families of the earth be blessed." (Gen. 28:13-14.)

Thus Jacob received the fathers' blessings, and ever after they were called the blessings of Abraham, Isaac, and Jacob. God changed Jacob's name to Israel. *Isra* means "ruling, prince," *El* means "God," so the name *Israel* literally means "ruling with God." God intends for the house of Israel—the family of Jacob—to receive the covenants of Abraham, Isaac, and Jacob and to rule with Him.

# THE SONS OF JACOB

The best recorded example we have in the scriptures of patriarchal blessings as we are familiar with them today is that of Jacob blessing his twelve sons and the two sons of Joseph. Through the designation in our patriarchal blessings, nearly everyone in the Church belongs to one of these tribes in the house of Israel.

First, in private, Jacob blessed the two sons of Joseph whom he claimed as his own by saying to Joseph, "And now thy two sons, Ephraim and Manasseh ... are mine; as Reuben and Simeon, they shall be mine. And thy issue, which thou begettest after them, shall be thine." (Gen. 48:5-6.)

Jacob then crossed his hands, placing the right hand upon Ephraim, the younger, to give him the favored or birthright blessing, and placing the left hand upon Manasseh even though he was the firstborn son. As patriarch, Jacob blessed the boys.

**Manasseh**, son of Joseph. He "shall become a people, and he also shall be great." (Gen. 48:19.) Moses later reiterated the blessing for the tribe of Manasseh, "They are thousands of Manasseh." (Deut. 33:17.)

**Ephraim**, son of Joseph. He shall be greater than his older brother and "his seed shall become a multitude of nations." (Gen. 48:19-20.) Moses later confirmed, "They are ten thousands of Ephraim." (Deut. 33:17.)

After Jacob personally blessed Ephraim and Manasseh, knowing he was about to die, he "called unto his sons, and said, Gather yourselves together, that I may tell you that which shall befall you in the last days.

"Gather yourselves together, and hear, ye sons of Jacob; and hearken unto Israel your father." (Gen. 49:1-2.)

This assemblage of Jacob's sons shows three similarities to the gathering of Adam's posterity. First, Jacob proceeded to pronounce blessings on each son, apparently in a public manner as Adam had earlier. Second, Jacob's telling "that which shall befall you in the last days" paralleled Adam's prophesying "what should take place even till the coming of Messiah." [6]

Third, in both cases we see a caring father, a grand patriarch, even at the end of life teaching his children and asking them to listen to his counsel. There is much to learn about fatherhood, patriarchs, and blessings by pondering these examples.

Because we belong to the house of Israel, one patriarch suggested we go to Genesis 49 to read the blessing given to the tribe to which we belong. As another patriarch put it, "We are those who should ... stand under the blessings of the fathers." [7]

The blessing Jacob gave to our tribal father flows through to us. In addition, approximately 200 years after Jacob's death, Moses gathered the tribes to give his final blessing. Moses' blessing went to each tribe as a tribe and therefore is important to those of us in each tribe. The following is a synopsis of the blessings given by Jacob and Moses. The sons are listed in the order they received their blessings from Jacob. Note that the order of the blessings is different from the birth order of these sons. (See Gen. 29:32 to Gen. 30:24 and Gen. 35:16-18; see Appendix I for a complete listing of both sets of blessings.)

**Reuben**, son of Leah. "Reuben, thou art my firstborn, my might, and the beginning of my strength, the excellency of dignity, and the excellency of power." (Gen. 49:3.) But he would "not excel" because he had sinned against Rachel's maid. (Gen. 49:4.) Moses added, "Let Reuben live, and not die; and let not his men be few." (Deut. 33:6.)

**Simeon** and **Levi**, sons of Leah. "I will divide them in Jacob, and scatter them in Israel." (Gen. 49:5-7.) For Levi, Moses said, "they shall put incense before thee.... Bless, LORD, his substance, and accept the work of his hands." (Deut. 33:10-11.) Incense indicated the priestly responsibilities of the Levite tribe.

**Judah,** son of Leah. "Thy father's children shall bow down before thee.... The sceptre shall not depart from Judah." (See Gen. 49:8-12.) Elder Bruce R. McConkie explained, "The sense and meaning is that when kingly authority was conferred in Israel, it would rest with the tribe of Judah 'until he come whose right it is' to hold kingly authority, that is until Shiloh [Christ] the great Lawgiver should inherit the throne of his father David. (Luke 1:32-33.)"[8] Thus, when Christ was born, He came through the tribe of Judah and was literally the King of the Jews.

Moses stated, "Hear, LORD,... and be thou an help to him from his enemies." (Deut. 33:7.) This blessing fit the tribe charged with ruling and protecting the people.

**Zebulun,** son of Leah. He shall "dwell at the haven of the sea; and he shall be for an haven of ships." (Gen. 49:13.) Moses said, "Rejoice, Zebulun, in thy going out." (Deut. 33:18.)

**Issachar,** son of Leah. He is "a strong ass couching down between two burdens; ... and became a servant unto tribute." (Gen. 49:14-15.) Moses stated, "[Rejoice,] Issachar, in thy tents." (Deut. 33:18.)

**Dan,** son of Rachel's maid Bilhah. He shall "judge his people" and shall be "a serpent by the way." (Gen. 49:16-18.) Moses said, "Dan is a lion's whelp." (Deut. 33:22.)

**Gad,** son of Leah's maid Zilpah. "A troop shall overcome him; but he shall overcome at the last." (Gen. 49:19.) Moses promised, "he dwelleth as a lion, ... he executed the justice of the LORD." (Deut. 33:20.)

**Asher,** son of Leah's maid Zilpah. "His bread shall be fat, and he shall yield royal dainties." (Gen. 49:20.) Moses said, "Let Asher be blessed with children; let him be acceptable to his brethren,... and as thy days, so shall thy strength be." (Deut. 33:24-25.)

**Naphtali,** son of Rachel's maid Bilhah. He is "a hind let loose; he giveth goodly words." (Gen. 49:21.) Moses stated, "O Naphtali, satisfied with favour, and full with the blessing of the LORD: possess thou the west and the south." (Deut. 33:23.)

**Joseph,** son of Rachel. Jacob said to Joseph, "I have given to thee one portion above thy brethren," meaning he received a double inheritance. (Gen. 48:22.) He was "a fruitful bough ... whose branches run over the wall." (Gen. 49:22-26.) Moses promised, "Blessed of the LORD be his land, for the precious things of heaven,... for the precious things of the earth and fulness thereof.... He shall push the people together to the ends of the earth." (Deut. 33:13, 16, 17.)

**Benjamin**, son of Rachel. He shall be "ravin [voracious] as a wolf; in the morning he shall devour the prey, and at night he shall divide the spoil." (Gen. 49:27.) Moses pledged, "The beloved of the LORD shall dwell in safety by him." (Deut. 33:12.)

As we study how Jacob, as a patriarch of old, blessed his family, we need to remember that "Patriarchs today possess the same power by which Jacob blessed his sons anciently. It is a power of revelation through which the Lord indicates blessings he has in store for you, personally." [9]

# BOOK OF MORMON PATRIARCHS

The Book of Mormon contains some patriarchal blessings given in the Biblical pattern of priesthood father to his sons. Before his death, in the pattern of Jacob, Lehi gathered and blessed not only his children but also his grandchildren. At the other end of the book, Mormon's letters to Moroni are, in a sense, a father's blessing in that they contain counsel and concerns for his son. (See Moro. 8-9.) In the middle are other examples such as King Benjamin who, we might say, gave a patriarch's blessing to his people before his death.

The "patriarchal blessings" given by Alma the Younger appear to be recorded and preserved in their entirety. The oldest son Helaman, who inherited the work of the Lord's kingdom, received a lengthy blessing comprising Alma 36-37. As is sometimes true with our own blessings, many of the details are to help him with his life's mission. A sample sentence in his blessing could fit in ours. "O, remember, my son, and learn wisdom in thy youth; yea, learn in thy youth to keep the commandments of God." (Alma 37:35.)

The youngest son Corianton received the longest blessing, one of much counsel and strong admonition to live the gospel and be faithful. As Alma put it, "I have somewhat more to say unto thee."

(Alma 39:1.) His exhortations filled eight pages of small print. (See Alma 39-42.) Corianton had walked a forbidden path, and this blessing undoubtedly influenced his turnaround.

Sandwiched between his two brothers was Shiblon, his brief blessing easy to overlook between their lengthy ones. But Shiblon's short blessing is the gem. Shiblon represents the many of us in the middle who neither run the church nor turn wayward. He represents those who receive short blessings. Did he feel unimportant because of it? How could he?—eight times in 15 verses Alma lovingly calls him "my son." These fifteen powerful verses give Shiblon commendation, testimony, counsel, and blessing—all that he needed.

Alma begins with "I trust that I shall have great joy in you… I have had great joy in thee already." (Alma 38:2-3.) His mission statement is a simple "continue to teach." (Alma 38:10.) He ends with "may the Lord bless your soul, and receive you at the last day into his kingdom, to sit down in peace." (Alma 38:15.)

Eventually Shiblon became the keeper of the sacred records after his brother Helaman. "And he was a just man, and he did walk uprightly before God; and he did observe to do good continually, to keep the commandments of the Lord his God." (Alma 63:2.) There was nothing wrong with being "lost in the middle" or receiving a short blessing. He received all the joyous blessings it promised, and more. What an example for us.

# PATRIARCHS TO
# THE CHURCH

The hereditary Patriarchal Order of the Priesthood is not functioning today. Early in latter-day Church history, the office of Patriarch to the Church was established as a beginning toward restoration of all things. Designating a patriarch provided an avenue whereby we, as modern day people of God, can receive our blessings as did His people of old. The Patriarch to the Church had overall jurisdiction and could give patriarchal blessings to any properly recommended member regardless of location. This office, like its priesthood pattern, followed a lineage.

Joseph Smith taught, "AN EVENGELIST [sic.] is a Patriarch, even the oldest man of the blood of Joseph or of the seed of Abraham. Wherever the Church of Christ is established in the earth, there should be a Patriarch for the benefit of the posterity of the Saints, as it was with Jacob in giving his patriarchal blessing unto his sons."[10] As the Church grew and stakes were created, patriarchs were ordained to function within the stake where they were sustained. These are the patriarchs as we know them today.

Eventually, when the Patriarchal Order of the Priesthood is again operating, natural fathers will serve as true patriarchs to their families, including giving them blessings. In the meantime, increasing emphasis is now put on fathers giving blessings to their children. At the same time, we have access to blessings through a properly ordained, set apart, and sustained patriarch who is entitled to give us a patriarchal blessing as of old. This system allows all, whether we have a member or worthy father or not, to enjoy the blessings our Eternal Patriarch desires to give us.

The following were ordained as Patriarchs to the Church.

**Joseph Smith, Sr.**—ordained December 18, 1833 at age 62 and served until his death September 14, 1840.

The prophet Joseph Smith ordained his father, Joseph Smith, Sr., as the first patriarch in this dispensation. Through revelation Joseph Smith declared his father held "the right of Patriarchal Priesthood, even the keys of that ministry; ... holding the keys of the patriarchal Priesthood over the kingdom of God on earth ... and he shall sit in the general assembly of Patriarchs, even in council with the Ancient of Days [Adam]."[11]

In proper order, "Joseph Smith, Sen., held this right by virtue of the fact that he was the legal heir, or first born, in the line of descent from Joseph, son of Jacob."[12]

**Hyrum Smith**, eldest living son at death of Joseph Smith, Sr.— ordained January 24, 1841 at age 40 and served until his death June 27, 1844.

Before dying, Father Smith gave a blessing to Hyrum, saying, "I now seal upon your head the patriarchal power, and you shall bless the people."[13]

The Lord confirmed this when He said:

> My servant Hyrum may take the office of Priesthood and Patriarch, which was appointed unto him by his father, by blessing and also by right;

> That from henceforth he shall hold the keys of the patriarchal blessings upon the heads of all my people. (D&C 124:91-92.)

Five days later, Joseph ordained his brother. We get a glimpse into Nauvoo life with the following newspaper item:

> The brethren are hereby notified that our well beloved brother, Hyrum Smith, Patriarch of the church, has erected a comfortable office, opposite his dwelling house, where himself together with his scribe and recorder (James Sloan,) will attend regulary [sic.] every Monday, Wednesday, and Friday ... to perform the duties of his high and holy calling.

> A copy of the blessings can be received immediately after being pronounced so that the brethren who live at a distance can have it to take with them.[14]

**William B. Smith**, last surviving brother of Hyrum Smith—ordained May 24, 1845 at age 34 and served until October 6 of that year.

Several months after Hyrum's martyrdom, *The Times and Seasons* reported:

> We have just received a communication from Elder William Smith, the only surviving brother of Joseph, and one of the Quorum of the Twelve....

> It will be his privilege when he arrives, to be ordained to the office of patriarch to the church, and to occupy the place that his brother Hyrum did. [15]

William was ordained by the Twelve and gave some patriarchal blessings, but he was rejected instead of sustained at the conference on October 6, 1945. Thirteen days later he was excommunicated. Because he was never sustained, he is often omitted from historical lists.

**Asahel Smith**, brother of Joseph Smith, Sr.—acted as Patriarch to the Church for three years from 1845 to 1848. Because he was never sustained, he is omitted from historical lists.

**John Smith,** brother of Joseph Smith, Sr.—ordained January 1, 1849 at age 67 and served until his death May 23, 1854.

As patriarch, John Smith wrote a letter to the Saints giving "some fatherly counsel." He encouraged those abroad to come to Salt Lake City so that, among other reasons, "I may lay my hands upon you and give you a Patriarchal blessing." [16]

He concluded with a blessing:

> And I say to the Saints, that by the power of the Holy Priesthood vested in me, as Patriarch, I bless you; and I say unto you,—Be faithful, and you shall be blessed in your basket and your store; you shall have all blessings which were promised to Abraham, Isaac, and Jacob; and the Lord will preserve you as in the hollow of his hand, and no power shall stay the work, for everything that shall be brought against it will fail. [17]

**John Smith,** oldest son of Hyrum Smith and wife Jerusha Barden—ordained February 18, 1855 at age 22 and served until his death November 6, 1911.

He was not ordained following his father's death because he was only eleven years old at the time. During his 56 years of service, he gave nearly 21,000 patriarchal blessings.

**Hyrum Gibbs Smith,** oldest son of John Smith's oldest son— ordained May 9, 1912 at age 32 and served until his death February 4, 1932.

**Nicholas G. Smith**—served as Acting Patriarch from 1932 to 1934.

**George F. Richards**—served as Acting Patriarch from 1937 to 1942.

**Joseph F. Smith,** great-grandson of Hyrum Smith and wife Mary Fielding—ordained October 8, 1942 at age 43 and served until he was released for ill health October 6, 1946.

**Eldred Gee Smith,** oldest son of Hyrum Gibbs Smith (great-great-grandson of Hyrum Smith)—ordained April 10, 1947 at age 40 and served until October 6, 1979 when he was released and received emeritus status.

In early Church history, members in areas without organized stakes, and therefore without ordained stake patriarchs, traveled to Salt Lake City to receive blessings from the Patriarch to the Church. By 1976 the situation had changed. A *Church News* article featuring then-patriarch Eldred G. Smith reported, "As the Church has continued to grow and the number of stakes increased ... his demands have decreased. As a result, he goes into the missions."[18]

By the time Eldred G. Smith was granted emeritus standing, every state in the United States had stakes with local patriarchs. Other countries also had organized stakes. Thus the people went to patriarchs closer to home instead of traveling to Salt Lake City to get a blessing. By February of 1996 more members resided outside the United States than within. These members increasingly receive patriarchal blessings in their own nations and languages.

# FATHERS AS PATRIARCHS

For now, patriarchal blessings are both a remnant of and a reminder of the patriarchal form of government. Taken literally, "a patriarchal blessing means a father's blessing. A patriarch is literally a paternal ruler. That is what the word means, and any father in the Church who holds the higher priesthood, may, in the authority of that priesthood give unto his child a blessing, and that is a patriarchal blessing, in that it is a father's blessing."[19]

President John Taylor said, "Every father, after he has received his patriarchal blessing, is a patriarch to his own family, and has the right to confer patriarchal blessings upon his family; which blessings will be just as legal as those conferred by any patriarch of the church: in fact it is his right; and a patriarch in blessing his children, can only bless as his mouthpiece."[20]

Joseph Fielding Smith commented, "The statement of President John Taylor is true with this qualification: The father must hold the Melchizedek Priesthood, that is, have the office of an elder, seventy, or high priest."[21] He added,

*The privilege of giving these blessings, of course, is limited to the immediate members of the family. ...*

*In my opinion, a father will be better qualified to give such blessings if he has been to the temple and had his wife and children sealed to him. There would be no need for a father to get a recommend from the mission president or stake president in order to bless his own child. However, the father should use discretion in giving such blessings, and they should be confined to members of his family who are members of the Church.*[22]

However, these blessings would not declare lineage. For now, that prerogative remains with an ordained stake patriarch. We can look forward to a time when the patriarchal form of government returns and fathers again bless their families as patriarchal leaders.

*We know that "Gospel laws and gospel ordinances are eternal. They are the same in all ages and on all worlds. During the Millennium ... at the appropriate time each person will receive his patriarchal blessing, we suppose from the natural patriarch who presides in his family, as it was in Adamic days and as it was when Jacob blessed his sons."*[23]

## SOURCES

1. Joseph Fielding Smith, comp., *Teachings of the Prophet Joseph Smith*, Salt Lake City: Deseret Book Co., 1977, p. 158.

2. See *Journal of Discourses*, vol. 16, p. 47.

3. *Journal of Discourses*, vol. 17, p. 188.

4. *Journal of Discourses*, vol. 11, p. 241; see D&C 107:56-57.

5. Joseph Fielding Smith, comp., *Teachings of the Prophet Joseph Smith*, Salt Lake City: Deseret Book Co., 1977, p. 159.

6. *Journal of Discourses*, vol. 11, p. 241.

7. Carl Ringger, "What Are the Requirements in Preparing for a Patriarchal Blessing?" *New Era*, Apr. 1972, p. 11.

8. Bruce R. McConkie, *Mormon Doctrine*, Salt Lake City: Bookcraft, 1979, 2nd ed., p. 710.

9. "Q&A" *New Era*, Mar. 1992, p. 19.

10. *History of the Church*, Salt Lake City: Deseret Book Co., 1946, vol. 3, p. 381.

11. Joseph Fielding Smith, comp., *Teachings of the Prophet Joseph Smith*, Salt Lake City: Deseret Book Co., 1977, pp. 38-39.

12. Joseph Fielding Smith, "Presiding Patriarchs," *Improvement Era*, 38:216.

13. Hyrum M. Smith and Janne M. Sjodahl, *Doctrine and Covenants Commentary*, (rev. ed.) Salt Lake City: Deseret Book Co., 1968, p. 786.

14. *Times and Seasons*, Nov. 1, 1841, p. 585.

15. *Times and Seasons*, Dec. 1, 1844. p. 727.

16. *Millennial Star* 3:98, Apr. 1, 1852.

17. *Ibid.*, pp. 99-100.

18. Jack E. Jarrard, "Calling of Patriarch Is To Bless Fellowmen," *Church News*, 29 May 1976, p. 6.

19. Joseph F. Smith, *Conference Report*, Oct. 1944, p. 111.

20. John Taylor, *The Gospel Kingdom*, annotated by G. Homer Durham, Salt Lake City: Deseret Book Co., 1944, 2nd ed., p. 146.

21. Joseph Fielding Smith, *Answers to Gospel Questions*, Salt Lake City: Deseret Book Co., 1966, vol. 3, p. 199.

22. *Ibid.*, pp. 199-200.

23. Bruce R. McConkie, *The Millennial Messiah*, Salt Lake City: Deseret Book Co., 1982, p. 673.

# CHAPTER 4

## Appreciating Your Lineage

## VALUE AND PURPOSE

How much do we understand the value of lineage? The Lord gave it immense value and purpose when He spoke of priesthood coming through lineage. He said:

> Therefore, thus said the Lord unto you, with whom the priesthood hath continued through the lineage of your fathers—
>
> For ye are lawful heirs, according to the flesh, and have been hid from the world with Christ in God—
>
> Therefore your life and the priesthood have remained, and must needs remain through you and your lineage until the restoration of all things spoken by the mouths of all the holy prophets since the world began. (D&C 86:8-10; emphasis added.)

So we are entitled to the priesthood because of our lineage. We are "heirs" because this lineage is "according to the flesh." Obviously the Lord thinks our lineage is important.

Eldred G. Smith, the last Presiding Patriarch to the Church, said a member is "entitled to receive a … declaration of the tribe of Israel through which his blessings shall come."[1] Priesthood is part of these blessings. Also, through our lineage "the promises of inheritance shall come, even as assignments to the inheritances to ancient Israel."[2] Thus, we will receive both our blessings and our inheritance through our lineage in the same way the original twelve tribes did. The promised inheritance ultimately becomes an expanse of "Promised Land" in our Father's kingdom.

For now, our lineage, our abilities, and our assignments appear to be intertwined. One woman said, "My feelings in my desire to know my lineage is that there are special things that we're assigned to do. I think we earned this and were given this in the pre-existence. I think there's a specific reason why we do what we do. I think we're assigned in some way for some purpose." (N.S.)

A father with children from three different tribes said, "It's my opinion that we're of particular tribes because of an assignment. Different tribes have different ways of doing things." (S.R.)

The idea of connecting lineage with assignment is verified by Joseph F. Smith, a former Patriarch to the Church.

> *I am of the opinion that that means much more than simply a declaration of fact....*

> *Certainly this declaration of lineage is a more important thing than simply giving an individual a psychological satisfaction as to his heritage.*

> *I believe that a declaration of lineage, by the authority of the priesthood is also a declaration of, and an assignment to, a responsibility. When one has his lineage declared, he is given a responsibility to fulfil, according to that heritage.*[3]

Knowing our lineage gives us a sense of position, promise, and purpose within the family of God.

# SEALING ORDINANCE

Elder Alvin R. Dyer wrote, "But, what is more important, the blessing contains a sealing by the designation of tribal assignment in the house of Israel. Without this the blessing given would be no more than an ordinary blessing at the hands of one who holds the priesthood."[4] Have we thought of the declaration of our lineage in this way—as a "sealing" to an eternal family? This assignment of heritage carries eternal import.

Elder Dyer continued, "But, with a place designated in the house of Israel, the blessing becomes more effectively a patriarchal sealing which does not terminate in mortality."[5] In other words, when the patriarch declares lineage, he designates or seals an individual as a member of the family of Abraham, Isaac, and Jacob. That person's righteous posterity can then inherit claim to the same promises.

Elder Dyer emphasized, "Man can be numbered in one of the divisions of the house of Israel only by the sealing of the patriarchal priesthood."[6] This shows us the significance of our patriarchal blessings and why the lineage must be given. We see there is more to it than learning who we are through revelation—which is the only way we can bridge the "pedigree gap" to our ancient family. In addition he explained, "Those of each tribe will be given their lineage distinction by patriarchal sealing, and all will be sealed, one to another, that they may be gathered to the land of their inheritance."[7]

This "patriarchal sealing" of lineage indicates an ordinance. Hyrum G. Smith, then-Presiding Patriarch to the Church, said a patriarchal blessing is "an ordinance in the Holy Priesthood, and is administered by the laying on of the hands of an authorized servant of God."[8] In addition, he wrote, "The closing is the sacred sealing of the Holy Priesthood. The blessings pronounced with all it contains is ... sealed forever, upon conditions of faithfulness to the laws of God."[9] A patriarchal blessing is indeed a sealing ordinance.

# IF LINEAGE ISN'T DECLARED

We have seen that inheritance comes through a lineage and that a patriarchal blessing is an ordinance intended to seal those blessings to us. A declaration of lineage, then, is a crucial part of the patriarchal blessing. If it is somehow omitted, the patriarch should give the person another blessing for that specific purpose. This is not considered a "second" blessing but is called an "addendum." The original blessing is a valid patriarchal blessing.

The need for an addendum happens. One woman wrote:

*When my husband and I were in the MTC before we left for our mission, I wanted to read my blessing, but I discovered I did not have a copy with me. I called my mother for a copy. She said, as she read it over, she realized my lineage had not been given, so she contacted her stake patriarch who indicated I was eligible to receive another blessing.... This new blessing was longer and very specific with no hidden meaning. (B.C.N.)*

A black sister reported that when she received her patriarchal blessing, she was uplifted and delighted, but somehow she felt everything was not complete.

*I thought my mind was doing tricks that I felt it was not completed. It kept nagging me, this feeling that I had to complete something. I said to myself, 'I have to talk to [the patriarch].' I felt like an orphan. I needed to know more.*

*When I talked to Brother J___, I received an addendum to my blessing that stated I was descended from Joseph who was sold into Egypt. After this experience I felt complete.*

*My blessing was reissued and officially recorded. The addendum was typed on after the first signature. (G.V.)*

When one woman's son was given the tribe of Manasseh and everybody else in the family was Ephraim, she looked at her blessing and discovered "no tribe. Mine told me I was a 'princess of the house of Israel.' I thought that sounded pretty good to be a princess! I never noticed there was no tribe." She went to a patriarch and got "one word—nothing else—just my tribe. I thought I'd get another chance for a blessing." (F.V.)

Perhaps one reason lineage is sometimes omitted is illustrated by the following two stories. One sister said she didn't get her lineage when she got her blessing at sixteen. "It bothered the daylights out of me.... My father was Jewish. Of course the real Jewish line goes through the mother not the father, but both his parents were Jewish... I went to the patriarch when my husband was bishop and asked him to read my blessing and tell me.... He put his hands on to see. He said, 'It's a very fine line here so go get a recommend.'" She never got around to it until leaving for a mission, and her husband "who was patriarch by then, gave me my lineage. I was of Ephraim."

Her brother also was not given his lineage in his blessing as a teenager. When he was in his fifties and became a stake president, a good friend of his was chosen as patriarch. The brother said to the friend, "Before you give anyone a blessing, I'd like to know my lineage." The patriarch said, "Give me twenty-four hours because it's my first blessing." Then he said, "Give me twelve more." He put his hands on my brother's head, then off, then back on. My brother said, "Why did you take your hands off?" The patriarch said, "When I was fasting, I got Judah. When I put my hands on I got Ephraim." (N.S.)

# BLESSINGS INHERITED FROM YOUR LINEAGE

One lady from the tribe of Joseph felt it was "more special because it means it's the lineage to Christ." False. Christ came as a direct descendant of Judah. This story shows why we need to understand what our lineage means. Our lineage is part of who we are. We also need to understand that every lineage has blessings and, without comparing, know that every line in the house of Israel is unique and important.

President Harold B. Lee said it is "very clear" that "those born to the lineage of Jacob, ... were born into the most illustrious lineage of any of those who came upon the earth as mortal beings." [10]

We can rejoice, regardless of which tribe we belong to. Think of this. "Your lineage is a 'blood relationship.' That makes you literally 'children of the prophets' with a noble birthright." [11]

Jesus is the One who said it, "And behold, ye are the children of the prophets; and ye are the house of Israel; and ye are of the covenant which the Father made with your fathers, saying unto Abraham: And in thy seed shall all the kindreds of the earth be blessed." (3 Ne. 20:25.) What a great privilege you have—to be directly descended from prophets.

# A SCATTERED FAMILY

The ten tribes of northern Israel, when conquered and scattered, became the "lost" tribes "in that they have not been identifiable as a recognized people since."[12] Because of the scattering, the house of Israel can be found anywhere and everywhere. Missionaries gather them. Patriarchs identify them.

In fact, we forget that Ephraim was one of the tribes lost but now gathering. We should not be surprised then that people from all the tribes are being "found." On April 3, 1836, Moses, who gave the tribes their blessings, returned "the keys of the gathering of Israel from the four parts of the earth, and the leading of the ten tribes from the land of the north." (D&C 110:11.) That process has been going on since.

A mission president in Mongolia found that his first secretary was from Reuben, then learned that his second was of Asher. As he interviewed missionaries returning to the country, he began asking them about their lineage. Those who had served in areas with patriarchs had received their blessings while on their missions. "Within eight or nine months I found every tribe except [one]," he said. He identified it later. "So all ten remnants are identified in Mongolia." (H.H.)

Although this reminds us of exciting prophecies of tribes coming from north countries (i.e. D&C 133:26), silently, but surely, forerunners from every tribe are already being gathered around us, wherever we live. (See chapter 6.) As the wife of another former mission president said, "They are right here among us." (T.T.#1)

"People are scattered here and there," a patriarch said. "I never know when one [of the less common lineages] will show up." For those who struggle to understand their lineage, he believes it's "because they don't understand, and because so much is said about Ephraim ... They are offspring of Heavenly Parents. What more could they want? ... The important thing is to live so we're entitled to all the blessings of Abraham, Isaac, and Jacob." (S.A.#1)

People of "lost" tribes "should not be concerned about it. They should get on their knees, pray to Heavenly Father, and see what direction, what guidance they receive." (N.H.)

The more the Church grows, the more we will see different tribes. To complete the family of Abraham we need all the tribes of Israel. We might paraphrase the message from the Apostle Paul in that we are a body or family in Christ; one tribe cannot say to another "I have no need of thee." Neither should one tribe say to another "I wish I were thee." Each tribe has a place. (See Appendix for examples.) Consider how it takes all twelve oxen to hold up the baptismal font in a temple.

# APPRECIATING
# WHO YOU ARE

A woman told how when she was growing up she had really not liked her name and had signed her papers in school with a nickname. "My patriarchal blessing said I needed to love my name because my parents had chosen it, and the Lord recognized me by it." (W.D.#1) She now uses her given name.

Similarly, we need to love and value the tribe to which we belong, for that is how the Lord recognizes us. One woman said that her sister was of Judah, so she had wanted to be of Judah, too. But her blessing "chastised her for it." She said they look alike and their husbands look alike, but their children are distinctively different. (R.C.)

Like this sister when she did not understand, occasionally others will not value the tribe to which they belong. We can realize that:

*The time we spent in the pre-earth life in the pre-existence was a great preparation for what our lot was going to be on this earth. Those of us who are of the house of Israel ... we earned that right in the pre-earth life because of our obedience and because of our valiancy. It wasn't just happenstance that you and I are of the house of Israel. We had to prove ourselves.*

*The house of Israel on this earth is a peculiar people and we were a separate and distinct group also in the pre-existence.*[13]

Let us recognize, appreciate, and value the blessings that come to us because of who we are through our lineage. "I am happy I am from the tribe I am," said a young Mongolian. "I am going to study more about it.... You need to study your family." (H.O.) Your lineage is a gift and a blessing. It is one way to know where you fit in God's family. Whatever tribe the patriarch declared for you, it is right for you, because that is who you are.

## SOURCES

1. Eldred G. Smith, "All May Share in Adam's Blessing," *Ensign*, June 1971, p. 100.

2. Eldred G. Smith, *Conference Report*, Apr. 1952, p. 39.

3. Joseph F. Smith, "Significance of Patriarchal Blessings," *Improvement Era*, Nov. 1944, p. 677.

4. Alvin R. Dyer, *Who Am I?* Salt Lake City: Deseret Book Co., 1966, p. 406.

5. *Ibid.*

6. *Ibid.*, p. 405.

7. *Ibid.*, p. 415.

8. Hyrum G. Smith, "Patriarchs and Patriarchal Blessings," *Improvement Era*, May 1930, p. 466.

9. *Ibid.*; see also Eldred G. Smith, "Patriarchal Order of the Priesthood, *Improvement Era*, June 1952, p. 425.

10. Harold B. Lee, "Understanding Who We Are Brings Self-Respect," *Ensign*, Jan. 1974, p. 5.

11. Julie B. Beck, "You Have a Noble Birthright," *Ensign*, May 2006, p. 106.

12. Richard K. Hart, "The Marriage Metaphor," *Ensign*, Jan. 1995, p. 26.

13. Ron Zeidner, "The Quest for Exaltation," Covenant Recordings, 1980, Audio Tape Cassette 1, Side A.

# CHAPTER 5

## Understanding Your Lineage

Stories help us understand. Here are some about the sons who head the twelve tribes of Israel. Here, too, you will meet some of your brothers and sisters of different tribes today.

# TRIBES THROUGH LEAH

## REUBEN

Reuben means "look a son." (Gen. 29:32, footnote b.) Leah was the first wife of Jacob and Reuben the first son. From Reuben's name we catch the excitement of parents welcoming a new child. The firstborn always holds the heartstrings of that moment, no matter what later years bring.

A woman said of her lineage through Reuben, "I think it's kind of special. It makes me feel wonderful. I'm proud of it. Reuben was the only one who stood up for Joseph. He saved Joseph." (W.S.N.)

Joseph's brothers plotted against his life. The Bible does not point fingers, so we do not know which ones conspired against him. Nevertheless, God's plan was to get the boy to Egypt where he could later save the family. Joseph openly forgave them all, as can we. We know Reuben showed courage to confront his envious brothers and said, "Let us not kill him." (Gen. 37:21.) His plan was to put Joseph in the pit to appease his brothers and to "deliver him to his father" later. (Gen. 37:22.)

Somehow he must have missed the selling of Joseph into Egypt because he returned to the pit later to find "Joseph was not in the pit; and he rent his clothes. And he returned unto his brethren, and said, The child is not; and I, whither shall I go?" (Gen. 37: 29-30.) We sense more than protection for a little brother; we sense grief. We can appreciate this all the more when we remember that Reuben was the firstborn son and therefore would have received the birthright had he remained worthy. Let us honor Reuben for his benevolence toward the brother who received the birthright instead.

Reuben also showed his character when the brothers returned from Egypt with the news that they must return with Benjamin. Reuben said to his father, "Slay my two sons, if I bring him not to thee: deliver him into my hand, and I will bring him to thee again." (Gen. 42:37.)

Like the woman above, others who are of Reuben can rejoice in it. A young married woman of Reuben said, "It means a lot ... I was told he's the one who lost the birthright [but] I went to the scriptures and found neat things. For one thing, he saved Joseph.... It helped me to know what he was like. It was neat to receive ... I belong somewhere. It was just neat to know I have a lineage." (J.I.H.)

# SIMEON

Simeon means "hearing." (Gen. 29:33, footnote b.) Leah named the boy Simeon because "the Lord hath heard that I was hated, he hath therefore given me this son." (Gen. 29:33.) The verse implies that Leah prayed for this child, and a child prayed for is welcomed and cherished.

Simeon, with Levi, slew the Shechemites to rescue their sister Dinah. (See Gen. 34.) The only other personal incident known of Simeon is of him being selected by Joseph as the hostage while the others went for Benjamin. (See Gen. 42:19, 24, 36 and Gen. 43:23.)

According to research, "The tribe of Simeon had become largely assimilated with the tribe of Judah by the time of Rehoboam, and the term Judah generally included Simeon."[1]

A patriarch of three years knew he had given a blessing with a lineage of Simeon. A mission president who had served in Mongolia had found "more than one" Simeon as he had interviewed returning missionaries. (H.H.) Readers who are, or know of someone who is, of Simeon are invited to contact the author through the publisher.

## LEVI

Levi means "joined" or "pledged." (Gen. 29:34, footnote a.) Leah saw the boy as the way to be joined with her husband.

We see the blessings and responsibilities of the tribe of Levi in Moses' time. They were unique from all other tribes, "For they are wholly given unto me from among the children of Israel; ... even instead of the firstborn." (Num. 8:16.) Consequently, they did not receive a land inheritance but instead served in the tabernacle and received the tithes. In a real sense, in keeping with their name, the Levites were "pledged" to God in service and "joined" the people to God.

Moses was a Levite with the record carefully verifying that both his father and his mother were of the house of Levi. (See Ex. 2:1-2.) When the Lord called Moses' brother Aaron, He told him to bring his brethren of the tribe of Levi, and "they shall be joined unto thee, and keep the charge of the tabernacle ... and a stranger shall not come nigh unto you." (Num. 18:2.) From this we sense a unity in the tribe of Levi in priestly service.

Today we know that "a literal descendant of Aaron has a legal right to the presidency of this [Aaronic] priesthood, to the keys of this ministry, to act in the office of bishop independently, without counselors...." (D&C 107:76.) We also know that the Lord has "pledged" that the tribe of Levi will one day serve in their priestly role again. (See D&C 13:1.)

Although the Levites were not given a section of land, they were given cities within each of the tribal areas. This mixed them among all the tribes and in time throughout nations. Thus a 14-year-old young woman of Korean parentage was of Levi. A brother from the tribe of Levi said, "It is quite an honor, but I'm not sure what I need to do, not knowing what's in the future. There's a great deal of responsibility on the Levites when the time comes." (A.N.)

A sister who was a Levite woman, like Moses' mother, had the privilege of meeting with Elder Neal A. Maxwell while attending Brigham Young University. "He didn't give any insight into the women," she said. "He talked about Aaron. He told me if my sons are of Levi they could be bishop without counselors.... He also said members of the tribe of Levi will again offer their traditional sacrifice to the Lord as part of the restoration of all things.[2] ... I was so in awe of being in his presence.... so nervous I couldn't even breathe. I wish now I could go back and take notes."

This woman's mother was born in Ohio "Lamanite country" and her father was of German descent. The patriarch told her that "the inspiration came to him and he suppressed it. It wasn't until the very last thing that he said I was privileged to be of this lineage and was entitled to all its blessings."

At first she thought that the Levites not inheriting land was a "kind of punishment" but then she "realized they did the Lord's physical work on earth for Him as He couldn't be here." She feels that being of Levi is "a neat, special thing. It's not any different in daily life today, but my future responsibilities will be different." She would like to know more about the role of Levite women, whether they will be temple workers too. (H.A.)

# JUDAH

Judah means "praise." (Gen. 29:35, footnote b.) When Leah bore him she said, "Now will I praise the Lord." (Gen. 29:35.)

Those born through the lineage of Judah come through the line of the kings. They share heritage with the great King David and with the King of Kings, Jesus the Christ. It is interesting to note that in a system with emphasis on firstborn sons and birthrights, Jesus came through the fourth-born son.

Judah conceived the plan to sell Joseph. Perhaps the profit offered him a way to convince his brothers so he could save Joseph. Judah did show a conscience for he said, "let not our hand be upon him; for he is our brother and our flesh." (Gen. 37:27.) By these words he defended the boy's life.

He also, like Reuben, offered to guarantee Benjamin a safe journey to Egypt. "I will be surety for him," he said to his father, "... if I bring him not unto thee, and set him before thee, then let me bear the blame for ever." (Gen. 43:9.) This promise was tested.

Joseph commanded that his silver cup be hidden in Benjamin's sack of food. When Joseph's steward apprehended the caravan on its return to Canaan, he of course found the cup, and the group was forced to retrace their steps to Egypt. There they faced a stern Joseph, not yet known to them, who demanded, "the man in whose hand the cup is found, he shall be my servant." (Gen. 44:17.) Judah then pleaded for Benjamin's freedom, saying, "his father loveth him,... let [me] abide instead of the lad a bondman to my lord; and let the lad go." (Gen. 44: 20, 33.) So Judah offered to be a slave, even as he had once sold Joseph, to honor his pledge.

After Christ returns, there are promises waiting, for "the tribe of Judah, after their pain, shall be sanctified in holiness before the Lord, to dwell in his presence day and night, forever and ever." (D&C 133:35.)

A mother and her husband, both of Ephraim, had a teenage daughter from Judah. The mother said she believed her daughter was "of a great lineage to help her lineage, to teach her people about Christ and that He is the Savior of the world." (K.E.)

Echoing her sentiment was this insight from a man who, much to his surprise, learned he was of Judah:

> I didn't know much about the twelve tribes of Israel.... I couldn't wait to look up the blessings in store for those who belong to the tribe of Judah. It turns out the Bible speaks somewhat regarding the throats of my enemies being in my clenched fist, or something to that effect. It satisfied my seventeen-year-old mind at the time.
>
> I realized soon thereafter that I really didn't need to look in the Bible for my inherited blessings, though I'm sure it didn't hurt. Immediately following the words identifying me as being from the tribe of Judah, I am told that I have been given this blessing in order to help me teach the gospel to the descendants of Judah.

> *Well, one might have supposed that I would have received my mission call to New York or Encino, but no, I went to a very Catholic area of Chile. I didn't teach a single Jew, as far as I know. I was even searching for one on the plane home, desperately trying to fulfill my patriarchal blessing.*
>
> *Perhaps I will serve another mission one day, or perhaps I'll run into a Jew at work. That's just like Heavenly Father, to keep me on my toes. (E.C.)*

One man who grew up Jewish looked at who he is in this way, "I am a Mormon Jew. Rather, I now belong to the Church of Jesus Christ of Latter-day Saints; yet, the blood of Judah is coursing through my veins." (V.B.H.)

A sister shared her experiences with her lineage:

> *I was raised in an Orthodox Jewish home. Our prayers were all in Hebrew and girls are not permitted to have a Bat Mitzvah in that strict organization of Judaism, so I did not learn much Hebrew. During my childhood I truly didn't understand much about the reasons why we did what we did in our home and at the synagogue because we were Jewish.*
>
> *I actually learned more about Judaism's beliefs after I became a Mormon. I also grew more proud of my Jewish heritage after joining the LDS church. Contrary to my ideas as a child that most non-Jews hate Jewish people, I have found the LDS people to highly respect and admire the Jewish people. The Mormons and Jews are both so family oriented! I felt I simply added on to my original beliefs.*
>
> *I knew there was a great deal of intermarriage among the different tribes in ancient days, and before receiving my patriarchal blessing the missionaries even forewarned me that most Jewish converts to our Church are not from the tribe of Judah. I sincerely hoped and prayed I would be. It was something very special to me to be from Judah. Therefore, when I went to receive my patriarchal blessing, I was determined to only tell the patriarch that I was a convert, but NOT that I was raised in the Jewish faith.*

*You should know that I resemble my father's side of the family whose parents emigrated from Romania. I do not look like a typical Jewish girl. When the patriarch announced I was from the lineage of Judah, I felt tears well up in my eyes and a joyous feeling in my heart.*

*As we have raised our six children in the gospel, we have taught them about the Jewish religion. We enjoy celebrating many of the Jewish holidays, as Jesus himself did. As each child received his or her patriarchal blessing, they knew I, their mother, was hoping they would also be from Judah. Alas, not one of them was.*

*However, our middle daughter married a convert to our church. When he received his patriarchal blessing, we were all shocked to learn that his lineage comes from the tribe of Judah. So I am thrilled that I now have a child—even a son-in-law—from the tribe of Judah. Now I'm hoping that one of the grandsons will one day also receive a patriarchal blessing saying he's from the tribe of Judah.*

Interestingly, the son-in-law's family "hated Jews. They thought Jews were worse than the Mormons." So she, with her background, "helped him work it through." (H.S.)

It is true that people born and raised Jewish may find their patriarchal blessings tell them they are of another tribe. Here is another story, however, of a woman of Judah by both heritage and lineage.

*It's very humbling and kind of exciting at the same time to be of Judah. We had a Sunday School lesson a couple weeks ago where our teacher was talking about the responsibility Joseph had to take the gospel to others because there were other tribes out there, that this was the role of Joseph, Ephraim, and Manasseh. I went up to him afterward and said, "Where does that put me?" He said I was a woman ahead of my time.*

*I thought, "Wow! I've never thought of it like that." I've never met anyone else not of Ephraim or Manasseh. I've never met anyone else of Judah. It's thirty-five years since I joined* the Church. There are not that many Jews who have joined. Now it is all the more amazing to me that I managed to join the Church when I did. Given my family and my background, how I managed to be receptive to the gospel is a miracle, not only that I had the opportunity but that I was receptive.

I tell people I am an Hawaiian Jewish Latter-day Saint. I am the only member on the Jewish side of my family. I feel a tremendous responsibility to my ancestors. I have done some genealogy and was able to find that my father's line for generations were orthodox rabbis. We've found they came from Lithuania. We've done the temple work for some of them. Basically they did the best they could with what they had. They have accepted the gospel. This is very special and even more humbling. They've been waiting a long time. It's exciting but very humbling too. I feel I have a responsibility.

My mother was raised in the Jewish faith and is a descendent of Aaron. We're not sure, but oral tradition says she came from royalty in Tahiti. My father's grandmother's name was Cohn which means something to Jews. It's a royal lineage almost.

I have a letter my great aunt wrote. It says, "Your family tree [goes] back ... to Russia where the family originated. A most remarkable feature of this family tree is the fact that Chaja Cohn [a great-grandmother] was a direct descendent of the priestly family Cohen which traces its ancestry to the High Priest at the Temple in Jerusalem for over a period of more than 2000 years.... Cohn ... was the name of the High Priest in Jerusalem.

"It is historically true and historians have proved it that nobody ever adopted the name Cohn but it has always been carried forward by the male descendants of this family. They are quite wide-spread throughout the world. Even today at the services at the synagogues when people are being called up for the reading of the Torah, the first person so honored is always *a Cohn or a descendant of a Cohn, if one is present.*

*"Also in the Orthodox synagogues, even up to this date, if a Cohn (or a descendant) is present, he is honored by being called to the altar where at the end of the services he pronounces the blessing of the congregation with the same words which the High Priest in Jerusalem used to utter:*

*"May the Lord bless thee and keep thee,*

*"May the Lord cause his face to shine upon thee and be gracious unto thee,*

*"May the Lord turn his face unto thee and give thee peace."*

*I don't know if it's because I'm of Judah or not, but I feel like I have a really big cheering section on the other side. I get extra guidance or inspiration. There is very little documentation available to get temple work done. There is a question whether the records survived the war. We know they kept records. Now the Church is microfilming records in Lithuania.*

*In 1927 my grandfather, who was a pious rabbi in the top echelon, was praying in the synagogue in Jerusalem when an earthquake collapsed the building and he died. We can't get a death certificate for him.*

After these many stories, she concluded, "I probably don't appreciate my lineage as much as I could if I understood it more." (S.A.#2) Perhaps most of us could echo her sentiment.

(Note: In July of 1998 the Associated Press released a scientific study confirming that the Y chromosome of Cohanim/Cohen [Cohn] males was distinctively unique.)

## ISSACHAR

Issachar means "There is a recompense." (Gen. 30:18, footnote b.) The territory he was given for his inheritance "was, as it still is, among the richest land in Palestine."[3] Nazareth was within the territory of Issachar. Little is known of him or of his tribe. We may assume that one day he and his lineage will receive a recompense and inherit their blessings.

One woman knew but had lost track of a friend from the tribe of Issachar. Readers who are, or know of someone who is, of the lineage of Issachar are invited to contact the author through the publisher.

## ZEBULUN

Zebulun comes from the Hebrew word meaning "exalted abode." (Gen. 30:20, footnote b.) Leah said that with this sixth son now her husband would honor or exalt her.

The connection of Zebulun with an "exalted abode" is interesting in light of the following report. "One of my great grandfathers was … a brick and stone mason … and helped to build the [Nauvoo] Temple. He obtained a patriarchal blessing under the hand of Hyrum Smith (many of his descendants, including me, have copies). He was told that he was from the tribe of Zebulun…. He built many of the oldest houses, churches and commercial buildings in Provo, including the old Tabernacle." (D.N.)

One mother had an adopted daughter from Wales who was of Zebulun. "I know it's important to her," said the mother. "She is proud of the fact." (S.I.) A woman from Mongolia (who was from Ephraim) had a Mongolian friend attending BYU-Hawaii who was of Zebulun. An older sister who had served a mission in Venezuela knew of a missionary there from Zebulun. (F.V.) These diverse geographic origins are not surprising in view of the "scattering." Readers who are, or know of someone who is, of the lineage of Zebulun are invited to contact the author through the publisher.

# TRIBES THROUGH RACHEL

## JOSEPH

The name Joseph comes from Hebrew root words meaning "to add," "to take away," and "to gather." (Gen. 30:24, footnote a.) Each of these meanings played out in the life of Joseph. Although he went to Egypt as a slave, honor and power were added to him. He was taken away from his family but caused their gathering.

Those who are of Joseph, either as declared by a patriarch or through one of his sons, share in the blessings of Joseph. An early record showed an interesting aspect of this. "In a patriarchal blessing given to grandfather he was told that he was a direct descendant of 'Joseph, the Dreamer,' son of Jacob and that he had inherited the gift of dreams."[4] An older woman reported, "Mine is worded differently. It says I'm from Joseph of Egypt, then Ephraim. Your life is very similar to his trials. You have his gifts, a kaleidoscope of gifts. But with that comes great trials." (N.L.)

Most of the insight into the blessings and responsibilities of Joseph comes through the words of his father Jacob. Before Jacob died in Egypt, he said to Joseph, "God shall ... bring you again unto the land of your fathers. Moreover I have given to thee one portion above thy brethren." (Gen. 48:21-22.) So Joseph received a greater land inheritance than the others. This is sometimes called a "double portion." These portions were named after Joseph's two sons.

Joseph Fielding Smith explained what it meant. "When Jacob blessed Joseph, he gave him a double portion, or an inheritance among his brethren in Palestine and also the blessing of the land of Zion.... Jacob also blessed the two sons of Joseph with the blessings of their father, which they inherited."[5] In addition, when Jacob blessed Joseph's two sons, he claimed them as his own. The Joseph Smith Translation emphasizes the significance of this.

> And now, of thy two sons, Ephraim and Manasseh, which were born unto thee in the land of Egypt, before I came unto thee into Egypt; behold, they are mine, and the God of my fathers shall bless them; even as Reuben and Simeon they shall be blessed, for they are mine; wherefore they shall be called after my name. (Therefore they were called Israel.)
>
> And thy issue which thou begettest after them, shall be thine, and shall be called after the name of their brethren in their inheritance, in the tribes; therefore they were called the tribes of Manasseh and of Ephraim. (JST, Gen. 48:5-6.)

We get insight into the mission of Joseph's seed through Jacob's words. First Jacob acknowledged that God had raised Joseph up to save "my house from death." (JST, Gen. 48:8.) This was literal and physical because of the famine. "Wherefore," said Jacob, "the God of thy fathers shall bless thee, and the fruit of thy loins, that they shall be blessed above thy brethren, and above thy father's house.

"Wherefore thy brethren shall bow down unto thee, from generation to generation, unto the fruit of thy loins for ever." (JST, Gen. 48:9-10.)

These words give a sense and place of honor. But the heaviness of responsibility goes with it. Jacob continued, "For thou shalt be a light unto my people, to deliver them in the days of their captivity, from bondage; and to bring salvation unto them, when they are altogether bowed down under sin." (JST, Gen. 48:11.) The blessing and mission of the lineage of Joseph, then, is to bring salvation to his brethren.

Bruce R. McConkie worded it this way:

> Even as Joseph was separated from his brothers, for their ultimate temporal salvation in the day of famine and want of bread, so Joseph's seed, the branches of Ephraim and Manasseh known as the Nephites and Lamanites, were separated from their Old World brethren.... And yet again, in the last days the house of Joseph is separated from their fellows in Israel, as they build anew the Zion of God to which all Israel shall yet look for eternal salvation.[6]

Not knowing or not applying these doctrinal truths to herself, a woman who joined the church at twenty-one was "baffled" by her lineage. Here is her story of how she came to understand.

> I could not understand why the patriarch declared that I was of the seed and lineage of Joseph and failed to specifically delineate through which of Joseph's sons, Ephraim or Manasseh, I would receive the blessings. Was I of Ephraim or Manasseh? This question instigated my seventeen-year search for the answer.

> One morning I took my blessing from the drawer ... after a fast, and therefore, my mind was clearer than usual that day. As a result, several phrases that had meant little to me in the past suddenly cried out for attention. Of these passages, one in particular was unsettling. It stated that as a member of the house of Joseph, I would receive all of his blessings as well as

*my own. Again, my mind was racing. Did that mean I was of*
*both Ephraim and Manasseh and would receive equal portions*
*of these lineages? Was there something I failed to understand*
*in what was said? I had known of only two others who had*
*received the same lineage, both from different patriarchs. They*
*were as confused as I was about it.... That day I made an*
*appointment with a patriarch in my area.*

*It was an enlightening forty minutes.... I showed him the*
*passage; he showed me something about myself that I could*
*have never dreamed possible—an understanding of who I am*
*and where I am to go. (R.T.)*

## MANASSEH, SON OF JOSEPH

Manasseh means "forgetting." (See LDS Bible Dictionary, p. 728.) One can guess why Joseph gave this name to his first son. Was it to forget the sorrows of his early years in Egypt, a symbol of looking forward to better days?

The story of Jacob crossing his hands to bless Joseph's two boys is well-known. We do not know, however, why Manasseh received his blessing from the left hand while Ephraim, the younger brother, received the birthright blessing on the right. But one thing is certain—Manasseh did not lose any blessing to Ephraim because of disobedience, unworthiness, or rebellion. When the boys received their blessings from grandfather Jacob, they were so young that "Joseph brought them out from between his knees." (Gen. 48:12.) They were hiding behind their father. We know that Joseph expected Manasseh to receive the birthright blessing, for he protested to his father. Whatever the reason, Jacob did not divulge it, and the Lord sanctioned Jacob's action.

Reminiscent of two brothers in an Egyptian palace long ago, parents from Peru had two boys close in age—one was of Ephraim, one of Manasseh. Twin sisters, though not identical, received their blessings—one was of Ephraim, one of Manasseh. Variations of this happens again and again.

A couple was married. The wife was of Ephraim, the husband of Manasseh. As the older children began to receive their blessings, two were from Manasseh, one of Ephraim. The mother said, "It's been kind of a fun thing." She could see differences in common traits. "I can tell," she said. "I can't pinpoint it, but I just know" which tribe they are. "I can't say one has more faith or more intelligence than the other. I can't say one is more like me or more like their dad." (K.M.)

Similarities and inherited characteristics within tribes may be real. However, consider these two comments. One man of Manasseh said he'd heard "Manassites are the type that want to be frontiersmen, the type to take risks. It seems to be true." (C.O.) In contrast, a woman of Manasseh said she had read that people from Ephraim went out and explored and those of Manasseh were not adventurous but stayed and did home building. (N.K.#2) So much for generalizations.

Sometimes different designations within a family are not easy to understand, and not understanding can cause negative feelings. One woman who was the only child in her family from Manasseh said she "didn't fit" and felt like a "black sheep." "I'm so different from the rest of the family. I wasn't surprised that I was from a weird one," she said. (E.R.) A blue-eyed part-Cherokee Indian felt he got "lesser blessings ... the bad end of the stick" because he was of the tribe of Manasseh. He also felt he "didn't fit." (C.O.)

Contrast their hurt from misunderstanding with the feelings of this sister who at first "did not consider the importance" of her declared lineage.

> After several years in the Church, I realized that many of my friends were not of the lineage of Manasseh, as I am. This realization had an illuminating effect. I began to ponder the significance of my lineage, and as a result, I became enlightened to my connection to a role and a people that I was unaware of.

> Moses referred to the descendants of Manasseh as the "thousands," this being less than the "ten thousand" of Ephraim. I found a great peace in what I feel to be an individual uniqueness that I share with this small group of brothers and sisters. With a new comprehension of my legitimate claim to the blessings of the Abrahamic covenant and my own role of

*carrying those blessings to others, I feel that my lineage is an exceptional gift and brings me great personal comfort. I am very grateful. (D.D.)*

All of one man's family, including his parents and his own ten children, were of Ephraim, making him the only one from Manasseh. "When I got my blessing, for some reason I thought I was of Manasseh. It's because of my call to work with Lamanites," he said. He thought it would be with a mission in Mexico, but he did not go there as originally called because of visa problems. However, "I continue to work with those of Lamanite blood in [work] and church activities. It's been a special thing to me."

He believes that our lineage is connected to what we are expected to do. "Manasseh is not in as much as a leadership position as Ephraim," he said, voicing what many believe, "but Lehi and others were of Manasseh." (C.R.#1) One Manassite, a college student from Mongolia, is becoming a leader. He recently won an award giving him seed money for a business idea. His plan, to establish laundromats in a country without either laundromats or private washing machines, will make life easier for his countrymen. (B.T.)

A woman of Manasseh said Nephi "was 'born of good parents.' I would say that, too." (N.K.#2) Who could ask for a greater tribal brother than Lehi or Nephi, both prophets who saw the Savior? Indeed, both Manasseh (Lehi) and Ephraim (Ishmael) sailed the sea, inheriting a whole new land, a double portion, together.

Likewise, two brothers, one of Ephraim and one of Manasseh, were departing for a "new land" of missionary service. The older one of Manasseh had many questions about his lineage. When he understood its value, he said his personal "gas tank" went from empty to full. He remembered other pairs of righteous brothers, the older invaluable at the side of the younger: Sam and Nephi, Hyrum and Joseph, Aaron and Moses. In the promised land, Manasseh and Ephraim each received a land of inheritance—side by side.

This man saw that he and his brother, from two tribes, worked together as one. A man in his ward "said he had watched us. He said we compliment each other—together we'd be the perfect missionary companions. What one lacks the other makes up for. Before, I felt I didn't fit. Now I see it's almost like yin and yang. It becomes one. We compliment each other. We're together there for the same purpose." (F.D.)

His comment reminds us of Jacob blessing Joseph's boys—the only scriptural incident of two sons blessed together.

# EPHRAIM, SON OF JOSEPH

Ephraim means "fruitful." (See LDS Bible Dictionary, p. 666.) Interestingly this son was born and named before Jacob blessed Joseph to be a "fruitful bough." The son seems to have been early, partial fulfillment of Joseph's own blessing.

Indeed, Ephraim became a numerous people. Valiant Joshua was the head ruler of the tribe of Ephraim in his day. (See Num. 13: 2, 3, 8.) However, when rebellious Israel possessed the land of Canaan, there were "none who were more guilty of this offense than Ephraim, and because of this rebellion the Lord punished him by mixing him among the nations."[7]

But the Lord had a second purpose for scattering Ephraim's seed—the "blessing of the people of other nations with the blood of Israel." Joseph Fielding Smith explained:

> It is essential in this dispensation that Ephraim stand in his place at the head, exercising the birthright in Israel which was given to him by direct revelation. Therefore, Ephraim must be gathered first to prepare the way,... for the rest of the tribes of Israel when the time comes for them to be gathered to Zion.[8]

In terms of this, it is noteworthy that Brigham Young proclaimed, "Joseph Smith was a pure Ephraimite."[9] One writer called the Doctrine and Covenants "a record of modern-day Ephraim."[10] The Lord specified, "Ephraim is my firstborn." (Jer. 31:9.) It is, therefore, Ephraim's right and responsibility to "stand at the head to minister unto the others. The Lord has called him to this mission in this dispensation."[11] Thus, those of Ephraim are found in many nations and cultures in order to accomplish this work.

A lovely black sister from Jamaica was baptized, received her patriarchal blessing, and learned she was of Ephraim. So were members from Sweden, Russia, Armenia, Korea, South Africa, Japan, Chile, Lebanon and an East Indian island. A patriarch from Mexico stated that some of his family were from Manasseh but many were from Ephraim. A full blood Chinese brother said he was of Ephraim. He was the writer of the following letter, asking for an explanation of what is an often misunderstood issue. (M.T.)

**Question**: *My companion and I were discussing the lineage of the Israelites. I am a full blood Chinese, and have thought much of my lineage as mentioned in my patriarchal blessing. When I told my companion that my blessing said 'You are of the lineage of Abraham, Isaac, Jacob, and Ephraim,' he commented that I must not be pure Chinese. Since he has made such a statement, I have thought much about what is mentioned in the blessing. I will be grateful if you will inform me as to the relationship between races: Chinese, French, German, and others. I am particularly interested in this because I interpret the lineage literally and not as an adoption.*

**Answer**: *Evidently the patriarch had the right interpretation. The great mission that was given to Abraham was that he would be a blessing to the generations coming after him, and through him all nations would be blessed.*[12]

A woman with an obviously Jewish surname who was born and raised Jewish was of Ephraim. Being born and raised Jewish "does not necessarily mean you're of the tribe of Judah," she said. "My folks were from Russia and Lithuania. Girls were gang raped by the Cossacks. Babies born of Jewish mothers were declared Jewish. That's the law in Israel. They were declared Jewish so they could have a Jewish upbringing. It's not unlikely that somewhere in my line someone became with child in an unwilling fashion."

The patriarch, she reported, "seemed more startled than I was." Some years later she was talking to the patriarch's wife who said her husband had been "terribly concerned because he had not expected Ephraim. It was a real testimony to me that when the patriarch puts his hands on your head that it's of the Lord and is specifically for you. Talking to her was a ratifying thing for me, a real testimony builder." (O.C.B.)

The wife of a former mission president observed that oftentimes parents in the country where they served would be of Ephraim, as first-generation members of the Church leading the way, whereas their children would be of other tribes.

## BENJAMIN

Benjamin was named Ben-oni by his mother, meaning "son of my sorrow." (Gen. 35:18, footnote b.) But Jacob changed his son's name to Benjamin, meaning "son at the right [hand]" indicating the place the father intended for his youngest son. (Gen. 35:18, footnote c.) Later, we might assume that Jacob considered Benjamin the birthright son in place of Joseph whom he thought was dead.

To test his ten brothers when they first appeared in Egypt, Joseph required them to leave one behind and the others to return with Benjamin. In the drama that unfolded, we see the father's great love for the lad. "If he should leave his father," the men told Joseph, "his father would die." (Gen. 44:22.) Rather than jealousy, the older brothers showed protection and kindness to the youngest. Joseph obviously felt a special bond with his younger brother. "And he lifted up his eyes, and saw his brother Benjamin, his mother's son,... and Joseph made haste; for his bowels did yearn upon his brother: and he sought where to weep; and he entered into his chamber, and wept there." (Gen. 43: 29-30.) We sense that Benjamin was favored not only by his father but by them all.

A sister who was converted in England had a mother from Burma and a father from Italy. Her mother's family had Polish Jews in Russia. With this background, she was "very surprised" to learn she was of Benjamin. "I've thought about it a lot," she said. It "felt like something special. What, I don't know. Nobody seems to know what it means." She knew that "Benjamin's mother died giving birth to him. Benjamin was the one true, full brother of Joseph. The others were half-brothers. He was the only other one from the father's favorite wife." (E.N.)

Another sister from Benjamin said, "At first when I was young, I thought I must be a bad person, as everybody else is from Ephraim and Manasseh, because I didn't understand.... [Then] I felt like I couldn't be a bad person—look how beautiful my blessing is.

"I listened for my lineage," she said, "but the patriarch forgot to give it." She received an addendum to learn her lineage. Then, the patriarch "told me I had a very special blessing,... that he had never given the tribe of Benjamin to anybody, that he had never missed declaring the lineage before." She wants to know more what it means and said, "I would love to talk to someone from my tribe.... I hold it sacred to me." (K.T.#1)

She would be interested in another woman's story:

*I knew I was of Benjamin before I received my blessing. I knew I was not Ephraim. I'm not that kind of person. I knew I'd have to be Benjamin. My best friend is also. It's neat to be soul sisters of the same tribe.*

*I felt I was a little different and that my spiritual sensitivity was different from the norm. I always felt I had extra gifts and blessings from the Spirit. My patriarchal blessing confirmed a lot of that to me and made me realize I was special, made me realize I had a special mission in life. Language cannot communicate spirit.*

*... My patriarchal blessing confirms to me I was different and special.... It is an anchor to make decisions in my life. [I don't know] whether or not any of that had a bearing on being of Benjamin, whether my valiancy had anything to do with my tribe....*

*I always felt I was different. I have just as much right as anyone. Through worthy living I can receive inspiration.*

*My best friend is my best friend because she's of Benjamin. That's why we connected. That was before we got our blessings. I got to know her in seventh grade. I got my patriarchal blessing before she got hers. I was in eighth grade. She got hers at sixteen. Once we knew we were both of Benjamin that's the tie that kept us together.*

*We have common characteristics. It's hard to explain. There are not words to describe. Friendly. It's hard to describe. A spiritual kinship.... We just fit.... [One day] I was able to sense that something wasn't right. I acted on that intuition and was able to talk to her long enough to find out what was wrong and to help her. That's the kind of relationship we've had through the years.*

*I'm the only one not of Ephraim in my ward. The Gospel Doctrine teacher said 'all' were and I raised my hand. Exclusionary behavior is not appropriate. We need to accept each other and realize there are difference even among us. (S.R.D.)*

Here is her best friend's perspective on being of Benjamin:

*When I learned that Benjamin is the smallest tribe, I realized that's why I don't find a lot of them.*

*[Being of Benjamin] is probably why I'm a peacemaker. My friend's the same. When I think Benjamin was the smallest and was the key to reunite that family, it is very special to me. He was not involved in that jealousy but was trying to bring people together.*

*That's how I explain things with my family. I was different. I did not cause problems but rather tried to solve them. I was different. I could attribute that to being of Benjamin. It might be my lineage.*

*At first I thought Benjamin can never be leaders. It's the smallest tribe and does not stand out in a crowd. Then I learned that Paul the Apostle was a Benjamite. That changed things for me.*

*My friend [S.R.D.] is the only one of Benjamin I know. I have similarities with her. She was a middle child like myself. We both like to be a mediator. That's why we connected so much—we could never get in fights! (N.I.)*

A man from Benjamin said, "Ten and a half tribes were lost. [Judah] and half of Benjamin were not lost. I think it's special. Benjamin was very much loved by his father. I think that might say something about Benjamin. Through Benjamin I'm eligible for all the blessings promised to Abraham, Isaac, and Jacob the same as anyone else, conditioned on my worthiness." (K.N.#1)

Another Benjamite said he joined the church in a "really unique area with many from different tribes," with three of Benjamin including himself. "It was fascinating to me," he said. "The three of us had a common trait. I won't say what. I noticed something about us. I also felt a kinship between us.

"I have no clue what it means" to be of Benjamin, he said. "I just accept it. It doesn't bother me.... The scriptures talk of the different tribes. It will be important or of some significance some day, but not now. I feel one of the most important things we can do in this life is to become pure before our Maker ... I go back to [my blessing] to consider that." (R.I.#1)

# TRIBES THROUGH ZILPAH THE HANDMAID OF LEAH

## GAD

Gad means "good fortune. (Gen. 30:11, footnote b.) Leah named the child. Little is known of him personally.

One sister from Gad had the "good fortune" to be among the first of her people to receive the gospel. Her sister was also from Gad as well as some others from Armenia. "My blessing tells me where I'm from and why I'm here," she said. "There are blessings promised to my lineage and the heritage I have. It is an incredible feeling to know I belong to the house of Israel, a sense of pride."

She explained what she understood about the tribe of Gad.

*From what I know, Gad means a warrior. Gad made a special covenant to rescue his brethren from Syrian captivity which he did and he received blessings for it.*

*Gad in Hebrew means warlike [sic.]. They went to rescue their homes and families. He did defeat the Syrians, freed his brethren, and lead them into Ararat which is ancient Armenia. Blessings were promised his posterity to be a posterity of survivors, very strong and committed to be strong to their covenants.*

*That's why Armenia was the first Christian nation. In
301 A.D. Christianity was put as the state religion. That's
fifteen years before Rome did. (O.T.)*

A Bible dictionary entry on Gad tied into some of the things she
had learned about her people. "The character of the tribe is throughout
strongly marked—fierce and warlike—'strong men of might, men of
war for the battle, that could handle shield and buckler, their faces
the faces of lions, and like roes upon the mountains for swiftness.'"[13]
The LDS Bible Dictionary stated, "Their district lay east of the
Jordan and ... was given them on condition they went armed before
their brethren.... The Gadites, who were brave and warlike were
sometimes known as Gileadites." (LDS Bible Dictionary, p. 676.)

One patriarch met a sister from Armenia. "We knew immediately
that she was special," he wrote. "When I gave her the lineage of Gad
it went through me from my head to my toes like a bolt of lightning."
(W.D.#2)

# ASHER

Asher means "happy, blessed." (Gen. 30: 13, footnote b.) Leah
named the boy.

A famous Biblical woman of Asher, Anna the prophetess, greeted
the infant Jesus at the temple and prophesied of him. (See Luke 2:
36-38.)

A modern woman from Asher had two unhappy marriages
and divorces. The second was especially difficult with "so much
hurtfulness." Here is her story:

*It was such a rough divorce, I didn't want his name. I had
no reason to keep it. I decided to choose a name I liked. I was
past using a maiden name. I decided to use the name of the
tribe I was from. I had to register with the county and then
had to wait a year. It was worth it. It has spiritual meaning
for me....*

*When I hear my name I remember that it was the name I
choose for spiritual reasons. It helps me be a better person.*

*I'm part of the twelve tribes. I know which roots I go back
to.... Asher is one tribe of Israel.*

*When the time comes, we will all pull together. We need to remember we are all on the same team. We should teach our children and grandchildren about love. Look at Jesus and the example He set.*

*We're all brothers and sisters in Christ. It's like being on a baseball team. I'm on the team of Asher. He has us doing different tasks with different talents.*

*It helps me respect all the others. We should teach children respect. It reduces all the world to twelve tribes. We are all brothers and sisters, and it's our duty to be respectful and kind to each other.*

*My name helps me to try. Sometimes I get discouraged. My name reminds me if I follow through, the blessings will be there for me.... I found whether I was true or not, the gospel was true. My name means a lot to me. (R.A.)*

# TRIBES THROUGH BILHAH THE HANDMAID OF RACHEL

## DAN

The name Dan means "He has judged, or vindicated." (Gen. 30:6, footnote a.) Rachel named the child.

Samson was a Danite born for a purpose—to "begin to deliver Israel" which would vindicate them from their enemies. (Judges 13:5.)

Surely there is purpose, too, in our births and in our lineage. A mother said:

*When I went with my teenage son when he received his blessing, I had an interesting experience. The patriarch said to me, "You're from the tribe of Dan aren't you?" I said I was from Ephraim. He remarked that the patriarch probably had a hard time determining my lineage. He asked where the declaration was in my blessing—top, middle, bottom? I happened to be in the middle.*

*When my son received his blessing, he was from the tribe of Dan. We have eleven children—only one of the nine who have had their blessings is from the tribe of Dan. The rest are from Ephraim. (D.R.)*

A wife and foster-daughter told about their deceased husband/father from Dan. "Dan was a warring tribe, and he was that type of personality," the younger woman said of him. (H.A.) "As I recall, Dan was not a warrior but very set in his ways. A large man. I don't know where we found that information," said the wife. (M.N.) A Bible dictionary said that the Danites had a hard time wresting the land from the Amorites and Philistines, which explained "the warlike and independent character of the tribe."[14]

"My husband was a convert and didn't understand a lot. He talked to the patriarch and asked, 'How did you know I was from this tribe?' The patriarch answered, 'It was the direct word from the Lord.' He said it probably had something to do with pre-existent service that was given and had something to do with the pre-existence," the wife concluded. (M.N.)

A woman of Dan also learned that Dan was a warrior, "a serpent by the way ... that biteth the horse heels." (Gen. 49:17.) "The Dans are still that way," she said, "Fighting for the truth. I do that all the time—fighting for the truth." She was the first person baptized in Armenia after it got its own mission. "My father died. After six months I joined the Church. My father was always arguing. I knew that choosing the right was good. I could argue for it." (T. I.#2)

Being of Dan, she had "waited for thy salvation, O Lord." (Gen. 49:18.) She called her life before baptism "twenty-eight years dead life." "All my life I did not know about the Lord and how we were created. I began to think about things. My father did not want me to read the Bible." She was twenty-seven the first time she saw a Bible. "At twenty-seven years, my grandfather died. My grandmother was living with us. My grandmother came in my room. She said the Lord's Prayer seven times every night. I heard her. It was the first time I heard of the Lord. I didn't know."

When she got her blessing she had been a member a couple of years and had come to the United States. "It was the first time I'd heard of the tribe," she said. "All my excitement, Anna [her missionary friend, not her real name] had—excitement, happiness. 'Read this,' [she told me] 'you need to know who you are.'"

Her people "are very much into tribes over there." The people intermarry within secluded villages where they keep traditions. "The families are the tribes. A whole village can be a tribe." (L.N.#2) Could blood ties to tribes of Israel be a reason why her country has the highest baptism rate of eastern European bloc countries? Being a "first-generation" Dan, she is a link between the ancient prophets and the fulfillment of their promises.

Here is a testimony from a Dan who is a black male member of the Church and a native resident of Nigeria.

> My name is UKOREBI Francis Etim [oo-koe-rea'-bee, last name given first] from Nigeria. I am from the Enugu Nigeria District. I got my Patriarchal Blessing at the ending period of my full-time missionary service in the Nigeria Ibadan Mission which I served from 2001-2003. It was indeed a pretty great day for me and my missionary friend.

> Can I really explain in full details my excitement over my patriarchal blessing. I guess I wouldn't be able to explain in greater details if I am given all the time in the world. I love my patriarchal blessing so much for it points out my weaknesses and the things my Heavenly Father expects of me and what to do to achieve all the numerous earthly and heavenly blessings that my Father in Heaven has in store for me.

> I enjoy reading and studying my patriarchal blessing each time I have the opportunity of doing so; it's just like scripture to me, and I am very happy to know the tribe which I belong to which is the tribe of Dan.

> Lastly, I know that the man who laid hands upon my head and pronounced on me my blessing was called of God and was His mouthpiece; and I know of a surety that our Heavenly Father will never fail in His promise to me if I would be absolutely faithful in fulfilling my own part of the prediction.

# NAPHTALI

Naphtali means "my wrestling." (Gen. 30:8, footnote b.) Rachel named the boy.

One sister had the patriarchal blessing of a great-grandfather naming him of the tribe of Naphtali. "He must have been surprised," she said. "I was surprised. Why was he of Naphtali?" She thought he came from England but had not yet established the connection. (N.R.)

A woman with ancestors from Germany, Ireland, Scotland, and the Isle of Mann learned she was of the tribe of Naphtali. She was new enough in the Church that "I didn't know what to expect, so I had no idea it was unusual." When she found it was unusual, she "felt unique" in a good way.

"It's kind of interesting. There's not much in the scriptures about it," she said. "What there is is sort of symbolic. I was told to look right in my patriarchal blessing and that's where most of it would be." She listed two good qualities. "I do have those characteristics and so I do have those blessings." To anyone else from Naphtali, "I'd say, check your own patriarchal blessing because it is scripture and that's where you'll find the most information." (D.K.)

# OTHER LINEAGES

Other lineages are sometimes given. One woman was of Judah adopted into Ephraim. A sister from Columbia said, "I have two lineages. I'm of Ephraim with the blood of Manasseh in my veins." Her blessing spoke of the "union" of the two and the attendant blessings. "The patriarch told me it was very strange, and I was very privileged to have two lineages together," she said. (M.L.)

Another lady said she was of Judah, Asher, and Gad, and even some not of the house of Israel, but mostly Judah. (J.B.) One man was told he was of "mixed lineage." "You mean I'm not the only one," he said when interviewed. "That's good to know." (V.H.)

Yet patriarchs confirm that most of us are a mixture of tribes. The lineage declared in these cases is the dominant tribe. As one patriarch explained it, when we go back to our great-grandparents, we have eight ancestors and therefore the potential for eight different lineages in our genes. We would carry "the blood of all those eight. All would affect us. ... The Brethren say there are three to five tribes within most of us," he said. (N.H.)

"I'm one of the lost," said a man born in Germany. His blessing told him he was a "remnant of the lost and scattered tribes" without specifying which one or ones. He hadn't thought much about it, but his wife thought it "pretty neat." "It goes with the first part of my life," he said. "I've been adopted twice; I've had three sets of parents. I've kind of been scattered." He thought that sometime he would go to a patriarch to learn more concerning his lineage.

One woman had a copy of a great-great-grandmother's blessing showing her of the house of Esau until her "blood shall be changed." (T.Z.) Who knows if this is the same story, but another sister wrote, "We have a copy of my husband's great grandmother, Sarah Wills Gale, who is from the tribe of Esau. She was born in Ireland, emigrated to Australia, joined the church and immigrated to America in 1852; then settled in Beaver, Utah." (B.B.) Esau, of course, was the twin of Jacob and the grandson of Abraham. One black woman was "of Abraham." (V.H.F.) Another woman, of Japanese-American descent, was adopted into the house of Israel.

According to one patriarch, "five or six percent of the membership of the Church are not of the house of Israel. When they receive their blessings, they are blessed of the house of Israel, a statement about like that." As they join the Church, he went on, they are "eligible to receive all the blessings of Abraham, Isaac, and Jacob." (N.H.)

As a member from Lebanon said, "All the tribes are great." (V.L.) We, the House of Israel, are all one family. Gathering into the Church is like celebrating a huge family reunion. You hold an important place in this family.

# SOURCES

1. "Gathering Scattered Israel," *Ensign*, July 1998, p. 61, note 1.

2. See Joseph Fielding Smith, comp., *Teachings of the Prophet Joseph Smith*, Salt Lake City: Deseret Book Co., 1977, pp. 172-173.

3. William Smith, *Smith's Bible Dictionary*, Old Tappan, New Jersey: Spike Books, 1981, p. 261.

4. I. C. Leany, *Biography of I. Leany in Autobiography of Wm. Leany*, BYU-A, p.18.

5. Joseph Fielding Smith, *Doctrines of Salvation*, comp. Bruce R. McConkie, Salt Lake City: Bookcraft, 1954, vol. 3, p. 251.

6. Bruce R. McConkie, *A New Witness for the Articles of Faith*, Salt Lake City: Deseret Book Co., 1985, pp. 423-424.

7. Joseph Fielding Smith *Doctrines of Salvation*, comp. Bruce R. McConkie, Salt Lake City: Bookcraft, 1954, vol. 3, p. 251.

8. *Ibid.*, p. 252.

9. *Journal of Discourses*, vol. 2, p. 269.

10. George A. Horton, "An Indispensable Foundation," *Ensign*, Mar. 2002, p. 40.

11. Hyrum M. Smith and Janne M. Sjodahl, *Doctrine and Covenants Commentary*, (rev. ed.) Salt Lake City: Deseret Book Co., 1968, Sec. 133, p. 845.

12. Joseph Fielding Smith, *Answers to Gospel Questions*, Salt Lake City: Deseret Book Co., 1963, vol. 4, p. 36.

13. William Smith, *Smith's Bible Dictionary*, Old Tappan, New Jersey: Spike Books, 1981, p. 196.

14. William Smith, *Smith's Bible Dictionary*, Old Tappan, New Jersey: Spike Books, 1981, p. 128.

# CHAPTER 6

## Insights from Patriarchs

## THE OFFICE

Being a patriarch involves more than a calling or position; it is an office within the Melchizedek priesthood. Men who are called to become patriarchs are typically high priests who are spiritually experienced. Because it is an office within the priesthood, for the specific purpose of giving blessings, they normally serve for many years.

President John Taylor taught, "The Patriarchs have the gift of being prophets, seers and revelators, to reveal the mind and will of God and portray unto the faithful their future lives."[1] Describing Joseph Smith's father, Wilford Woodruff said, "when he laid his hands upon a man's head it seemed as if the heavens and the hearts of men were open to him, and he could see their past, present and future."[2]

Do we believe in the prophetic power of patriarchs? President Heber J. Grant stated that unless patriarchs are able "to give blessings which are fulfilled, then there is nothing gained by believing" in them.[3] He told stories from his own life showing such fulfillment. One missionary commenting on his own patriarchal blessing put it simply, "That's prophecy." (F.C.)

How do patriarchs get the ability to make prophetic statements? Personal spiritual preparation, of course, is part of the answer. But there is more to it. Priesthood power comes with the office. After ordaining a patriarch, President Harold B. Lee received a letter from the stake president's wife who had witnessed it in a basement room.

*"You walked over and put your hands on his head, and a light came from behind you and went right through you and into him. And I thought to myself, Isn't that a strange coincidence that the sunlight has come in just at that moment. And then I realized that there was [no window,] no sunlight.... That light came from somewhere beyond Brother Lee and went through Brother Lee into this patriarch."* [4]

"And so it must be," Boyd K. Packer added after telling the story. "Whenever a patriarch is ordained or pronounces a blessing, that same light, though it may be unseen, is present. It empowers a patriarch to declare lineage and to give a prophetic blessing, notwithstanding that he himself may be a man of very ordinary capacity. ... The office of stake patriarch ... is essential to the spiritual power of a stake."[5]

## THE CALLING

Until a few years ago, patriarchs were interviewed, called, and ordained by an Apostle visiting the stake needing one. Today the stake president submits a name to the Quorum of the Twelve Apostles who will then prayerfully consider before approving the action. A new patriarch is sustained during stake conference then ordained to this office in the Melchizedek Priesthood.[6]

A sample reaction of how it feels to be called as a patriarch was shared by G. W. Jensen. Elder Boyd K. Packer interviewed, called, and ordained him during a stake conference. After the ordination, Elder Packer spent ten minutes giving counsel before rushing to catch a plane. Brother Jensen was then on his own. Once, new patriarchs traveled to Church headquarters for a week of orientation including reading patriarchal blessings in the archives. Brother Jensen had one consolation—Elder Packer's promise of a book of help in the mail.

When the "book" arrived, it was six pages, mostly about details such as checking the recommend and recording the blessing. "Where does it say how to give a blessing?" he asked desperately. Then he realized, "I had missed the most important thing that Elder Packer had said. He told me it was between me and the Lord, and I was to live such a life as to be worthy." He also found comfort and encouragement in the Lord's promise, given through Elder Packer, that the words would come.

Another patriarch said the "handbook for a patriarch is the scriptures and the life of the Savior.... There is no warm-up. The first blessing has to be as inspired as the last." (R.V.)

The overwhelming feeling of being a new patriarch was also expressed by Urvin Gee who was ordained by George Albert Smith in 1936. Shortly after his ordination, a departing missionary called for an appointment. Having no idea how to give a patriarchal blessing, Brother Gee pleaded through prayer and studied and meditated. He decided on an opening sentence but still had no idea how to proceed. He had no instructions. He only knew the blessing must come from the Lord. The hour came. He had to begin.

> I began to repeat the introductory sentence I had decided upon. While I was doing this, although my eyes were closed, I felt that I was looking at a large placard on which was printed part of the blessing. I would read it and new words would appear. This happened a number of times. When no more words appeared I closed with an appropriate sentence, which I had previously decided upon.[7]

He never had a similar experience. After that Brother Gee said he began "choosing the words and forming the sentences, but relying upon the Spirit of the Lord for the promises and blessings. I am simply the mouthpiece of our Heavenly Father in giving patriarchal blessings."[8]

Another new patriarch, paralyzed for months by the responsibility, received permission from his stake president to write and use a model first paragraph. Then when he finally gave the first blessing, he put his hands on the young man's head, and "did not use one word of it."[9]

Perhaps the "granddaddy" of Church patriarchs is Joseph L. Petersen of Joseph City, Arizona. He recalls his ordination:

> When I was ordained a patriarch by Apostle Ezra Taft Benson, November 27, 1949, after he had ordained me, I asked him, "When will I be ready to give patriarchal blessings?" He answered, "You will know when you are ready.

*It may be three or four weeks, but you will know when you are ready." I immediately started praying and fasting and praying to prepare myself for this sacred calling. On Saturday morning twenty days after I was ordained, something came into me that changed me immediately. In a moment I was changed to know I was ready to give patriarchal blessings, and I was filled with a desire to bless others. The following day was Sunday. I gave four blessings that day, and I was led by the spirit of the Holy Ghost as I gave these blessings. It was the spirit of the Holy Ghost that came into me and changed me after I became sufficiently humble, and the spirit of the Holy Ghost has been with me and led me as I have given 1744 blessings. (Letter to author.)*

Turning his experience into wise counsel for each of us, Brother Petersen continued:

*Each one of us, as we were baptized and became members of the Church were given the Holy Ghost, and the Lord expects us to be humble and prayerful and read the scripture so we will be worthy to have the help and blessings of the spirit of the Holy Ghost.*

In the Bible, Matthew 7:7, the Lord gives us this promise, "Ask and it shall be given you, seek and ye shall find, knock and it shall be opened unto you." Then to make His promise more impressive, we read verse 8— "For everyone that asketh receiveth and he that seeketh findeth, and to him that knocketh it shall be opened." (Ibid.)

Then, in a gentle way, this spiritual man, guided by the Holy Ghost for more than forty years in blessing others, concluded, "I am 104 years old, and I will be glad if this can help others." (Ibid.)

# THE ROLE OF THE PATRIARCH

After giving hundreds of patriarchal blessings, Wilford J. Reichmann felt that being a patriarch is the most difficult calling he ever had in the church. "'It scares you near to death,' he said, as he spoke of the need to be constantly in tune with the spirit." [10]

A patriarch speaks for the Lord—this is the unique power and beauty of a patriarchal blessing. The deeper we root our faith in this truth, the more cherished and usable our blessings become. A girl confided, "While my patriarchal blessing was being pronounced upon me, I imagined that my Heavenly Father was there with his hands on my head saying the words himself." [11]

A young man described his experience this way. "The patriarch laid his hands upon my head and began to prophesy about my life. I could feel that it was all true and that it was really God that was speaking through the patriarch. I wept." [12]

An enthusiastic convert showed the role of a patriarch by sharing her experience. When receiving her blessing, she said,

> *I came to know that Heavenly Father truly does hear our prayers, and that he will answer them. Now, I always had a testimony of this but the experience during my blessing was so profound that it was seared into my soul. There were no visions or voices other than the voice of the patriarch, but I knew that Heavenly Father was talking to me through this righteous man. As he laid his hands on my head and proceeded to pronounce the blessing, I heard answers to questions that I had been praying about. There were four questions that I had been including in each prayer I said. The first four things the patriarch said were answers to these questions. But they weren't just answers using any words. They were the words and phrases I used when I talked to my Father in secret prayer. I knew this blessing was from my Father in Heaven, and I have always placed my trust in the things that are found therein. (L.P.)*

We realize, of course, that the readiness of the recipient plays a role in the patriarch's ability to convey the blessing. One patriarch said, "Their spirit has as much impact on the blessings as the spirit of the patriarch." (H.I.) In fact, as another wrote, "The spirit of the receiver unites very strongly with that of the patriarch while the blessing is being pronounced." [13] Yet another patriarch said he "can feel a certain love, a certain compassion, a certain spirit" he tries to identify in the blessing. (E.W.)

One man had requested his blessing as a convert at about age thirty. Now a great-grandfather with a lifetime of memories, he declared, "Getting my patriarchal blessing was the greatest experience I ever had!" Overwhelmed, he had shed "tears like a baby." (N.C.T.)

The patriarch told him afterwards, "It was one of the easiest blessings I ever gave. It just came through." The patriarch contributed his part, too. He was "certainly a spiritual man; he couldn't hear a word but never missed a meeting because he felt the Spirit there." Indeed, it is the patriarch's job to be so in tune with the Spirit that the blessing can "just come through."

How, then, does a patriarch prepare to give a blessing? One patriarch made this comparison:

> I heard Elder Harold B. Lee say, "Never prepare a talk, but prepare yourself to give a talk." It struck me forcibly how well that advice pertains to a patriarch—he cannot prepare a blessing, but must prepare himself to receive and give a blessing.[14]

A patriarch who had been serving about a year said, "One thing I learned real fast is that it's not the patriarch's blessing. It's Heavenly Father's blessing, and the patriarch is just the secretary. If the patriarch doesn't have the Spirit, it doesn't work.... I can be in the world, but I can't be of the world in any way. I've got to watch what I read and see. You can't do anything without the Spirit. It's not like a Sunday School lesson you prepare and give. It's preparing all week long, twenty-four hours a day, even if you only give one blessing a week. It's the most challenging calling I've ever had to have the Spirit and keep myself worthy." (N.E.) And he said that after years as a bishop, stake president, and mission president.

If ever a patriarch proved unworthy, the blessings he pronounced would still stand. One man told of this happening.

> Our beloved patriarch was excommunicated while I was on the high council. The stake presidency had great fears that the great number of blessings that had been given over the years would be felt less than they were, and people would want an additional blessing. The stake president reported that not one person out of several thousand blessings asked for an additional blessing. He stated that the people he interviewed

*had felt their blessings came through the mantle of a patriarch from the Lord, even though this man had not been living up to the standards of the Church.*

*I can personally say that the spirit was so strong when I received my patriarchal blessing through this patriarch that without a shadow of a doubt I know my blessing came from God. (S.S.)*

Elder Carlos E. Asay, while in the Presidency of the First Quorum of the Seventy, expressed the role of the patriarch and the recipient this way:

*By way of illustration, the patriarch stands with you at the starter's gate. He envisions for you the race that lies ahead. With the aid of his special gifts, he outlines the rules of the contest, he describes the challenges that will be faced, and he cites the laurels that may be won. However, you, the runner, must stay in the marked lane, abide the rules, cover the course, and cross the finish line if you expect to receive the victor's prize.*[15]

"The Lord is giving it," said a patriarch. "I am talking for the Lord, representing the Lord even with the pronoun 'I.'" (E.W.)

# TAILORED TO THE INDIVIDUAL

Another evidence that our blessings come from God is their uniqueness. One father, now a patriarch, noted how different his two daughters were in personality and how different their blessings were to fit them. The older daughter needed to be told what to do in specific detail which is exactly what her blessing did. The younger daughter who was independent to the point of getting her blessing without telling her parents "was told to counsel with her parents." (R.V.) His point was that our blessings are tailored to fit the individual; he was not comparing them.

"Never compare your blessing to someone else's" especially not siblings, said a patriarch. One blessing is not "better" than another.

We have "lots of common blessings, so a lot will sound alike," but they "come through inspiration. The commonality is the gospel blessings," he explained. (E.W.)

A woman who has typed patriarchal blessings for her father-in-law for fifteen years said that the patriarch has words he tends to repeat such as "indeed." Then she'll come across a word like "downtrodden" and say, "I haven't typed that word before. We all have our patterns of speaking. Even though the Lord is speaking, it comes out in the patriarch's way of speaking," she said. (A.K.) But each blessing is different.

# IMPRESSIONS

Without question, patriarchs receive inspiration in giving blessings. James Womack, a patriarch who had lost his hands and much of his vision in World War II, reported his experience.

When he first received the calling, he prayed that the impressions would be strong on his mind—and "they were so strong that I had to go back in a few weeks and pray that the Holy Ghost would lift them, because I couldn't forget them. The scenes, the thoughts, the ideas of those blessings I gave stayed stamped on my mind as if I had witnessed them."[16]

Sometimes patriarchs struggle with the impressions they receive. One patriarch told of this experience while he was giving a blessing to a girl he did not know:

*I had the impression to tell her to study and improve her God-given talent for music. Immediately there followed the thought, "Maybe she does not have any desire nor talent in music and I will be making a statement entirely out of place." So I groped for other thoughts. I received this impression a second time, and for the second time I put it out of my mind. As I slowly proceeded, all at once I realized that I had told her she should apply herself to improve her talent for music and it would be a blessing in her life. As I talked to her after the blessing was given, I learned that she had been discouraged in her music.*[17]

Wilford J. Reichmann, a patriarch in St. George, Utah, told of when he refused to give a blessing, even though the woman had the necessary bishop's recommend. He didn't have a good feeling about her, so he told her he couldn't give her a blessing at that time. He invited her to return the following week. She didn't show up.

Later, the patriarch found out that "the woman was not a member of the Church.... She had obtained the recommend from a new bishop who had not waited for membership records the woman said would be arriving from her previous ward." [18]

His impression had protected the sanctity of the ordinance.

# INSIGHTS ON LINEAGE

Patriarchs consistently affirm that the declaration of lineage is God-given. "When I was called as a patriarch many years ago, I was very concerned about declaring the lineage. How was I going to tell? The outgoing patriarch said not to worry about it. The Lord provides that information. He told me he once gave blessings to twin girls on the same night. The first one was of Ephraim. He started the second with no qualms. But he couldn't talk. He tried again and still couldn't talk. He said a quick prayer. Finally he gave a different tribe. They were not identical twins."

He told his own story. "Sometimes I don't know what tribe is coming up.... I've given quite a few of Judah, a Benjamin, and quite a few other tribes. A blonde lady was Manasseh. They are all given through inspiration." (N.H.)

"The pronouncing of lineage is strictly through the Spirit," confirmed another patriarch. "One time I was going to give a patriarchal blessing to a young man. The mother was Navajo and the father at least 50 percent Cherokee, so I had it in my mind 'Manasseh,' but the word would not form in my mouth and Ephraim came out." (N.E.) Most patriarchs can tell similar stories.

In contrast, many patriarchs also agree with the one who said, "Sometimes I get a strong impression of the lineage, sometimes even before the person comes." (K.T.#3)

Generally, however, patriarchs do not know the lineage until the Spirit reveals it during the blessing. Strong feelings can accompany this revelation. One patriarch said, "I gave a blessing in New York to a Jewish girl in 1962. I could feel the love the Savior had for his blood daughter. It was marvelous." (R.V.)

There are currently three main tribes gathering in the Church: Ephraim, Manasseh, and Judah. "If the patriarch feels the recipient is from another tribe, the patriarch is entitled to take his hands off and go pray about it," said a patriarch. (N.E.)

"The scriptures gave different tribes different blessings," another patriarch said. "The potential of those sons and daughters are about the same regardless of which tribe they are from. When blessings are given, regardless of the lineage, they give the same blessings. The blessings depends on how they live life." (N.H.)

"Ephraim has the responsibility for gathering Israel … [and] the responsibility for leadership," the other patriarch continued. "Each tribe without a doubt has its own responsibility to fulfill. All of them do." (N.E.)

"It always helps," he said, "to know who you are and where you came from and whose blood is flowing in your veins. … You want to know where you belong." (N.E.)

# WHEN THE WORDS WON'T COME

A story is told of two boys who went together to receive their blessings. The patriarch knew one of them personally and in greeting the youth he said, "I have a wonderful blessing for you."

He blessed the other boy first. Then he laid his hands on the head of the boy for whom he had said he had a wonderful blessing, and he found he could not give him a blessing at all. The words just would not come. Finally he had to say, "You will have to come back some other time."

The Lord let that patriarch know that no patriarch has a blessing for anybody. The blessings are from the Lord.[19]

One patriarch learned another lesson from the Lord with one of the first blessings he gave. When a young man called for an appointment, the patriarch felt uncomfortable; he felt even more uncomfortable when the youth came. He struggled trying to give the blessing—the words just would not come. When he checked the tape, for some unexplainable reason only the first few sentences had recorded. Another appointment was made; the youth arrived. Again the patriarch felt uncomfortable. This time the young man said, "I know why the blessing didn't record," and he confessed that he had sinned. The patriarch added, "I learned that when the words don't come, the influence of the Lord is not there." (H.A.K.)

# FROM THE HEARTS
# OF PATRIARCHS

Patriarchs feel the sacredness of their calling. They are eager for us to use our blessings to guide our lives. From their vantage point they offer wisdom and insight.

"In order to understand your blessing, you have to understand the blessings of Abraham, Isaac, and Jacob," said one. "The scriptures say you must be like Abraham." (R.V.) "Read in Genesis and the book of Abraham about patriarchal blessings," said another. "The more we know, the more we appreciate it." (N.E.) (See chapter 3.)

A third said, "As we join the Church, we receive all the blessings of Abraham, Isaac, and Jacob. Conversely when we're unfaithful, we don't receive the blessings. The patriarchal blessing [becomes] just a piece of paper with a bunch of words on it." (N.H.) Also speaking of a life not lived right, another said blessings are "not designed to straighten out your life. Sometimes that's the reason people want them." (H.I.)

One patriarch offered this insight, "Blessings are feelings. Read for feelings rather than words. Blessings carry the Spirit.... A scripture says when a man speaketh by the Holy Ghost, the Holy Ghost carries it into the heart of men. (See 2 Ne. 33: 1.) So if you have clean heart and hands when you read it, a powerful Spirit goes with it." (R.V.)

"Patriarchal blessings are meant for our lifetime and hereafter," he commented. "Dallin H. Oaks in General Conference said, 'In our eternal journey, the resurrection is the mighty milepost that signifies the end of mortality and the beginning of immortality.' That opened my eyes to what our blessings can mean." (R.V.) [20]

A woman with two brothers who are patriarchs said, "They say the blessing is not to tell you what your life will be but to tell you where you fit." (L.E.)

"It is not by chance you are who you are," said a patriarch. "Your ancestors crossed the Jordan River. Two-thirds of Europe died in the Black Plague." As Israel gathers and marries and comes together, "the blood becomes purer and purer and stronger and stronger in the children. The world [now] has some of the choicest souls." Then he added, "These blessings are sealed. They're yours." (R.V.)

# THE JOY OF A PATRIARCH

Patriarchs enjoy many rewarding experiences. "Youth come with great expectations, sometimes a little trepidation. Youth are being prepared for a mighty work. It is thrilling to hear some of their experiences in seminary. It is thrilling to hear some of their problems and how they turn to Heavenly Father. They have tears of joy and gratitude in their eyes when they leave." (H.A.K.)

A patriarch can go to a reading room in Salt Lake City and read blessings in a collection from the last seventy years. A patriarch who did so said, "The spirit of them overwhelms you. They are from God. They are so sacred. I felt this great spirit about them. My eyes opened to how the Lord deals with His children." The beauty of the language, spoken through the Holy Ghost, struck him as the "tongue of angels." (R.V.)

Patriarchs feel joy in their calling. A patriarch in Mexico deals with the physical effects of aging, but, he says, "when my children ask me, 'Are you giving blessing, Dad?' I tell them, 'No, I'm receiving blessings.'"[21]

"One of the great things of being a patriarch," said one, "is getting a vision of the greatness of God's children." (H.A.K.)

# SOURCES

1. *Conference Report*, Apr. 1902, p. 44.

2. *Journal of Discourses*, vol. 12, p. 276.

3. *Conference Report*, Apr. 1935, p.12.

4. *The Teachings of Harold B. Lee*, ed. Clyde J. Williams, 1996, pp. 488-489; as quoted by Boyd K. Packer, "The Stake Patriarch," *Ensign*, Nov. 2002, p. 45.

5. Boyd K. Packer, "The Stake Patriarch," *Ensign*, Nov. 2002, p. 45.

6. See Boyd K. Packer, "The Stake Patriarch," *Ensign*, Nov. 2002, p. 42.

7. J. M. Heslop, "Stake Patriarch, 92, Loves Church Job Over Any Other Duty," *Church News*, 16 Mar. 1974, p. 13.

8. *Ibid.*

9. Boyd K. Packer, "The Stake Patriarch," *Ensign*, Nov. 2002, p. 44.

10. "Being Patriarch Is a Humbling Call," *Church News*, 30 Nov. 1974, p. 10.

11. "Q&A" *New Era*, Mar. 1992, p. 19.

12. "Q&A" *New Era*, Mar. 1992, p. 18.

13. Elmo J. Bergeson, "The Patriarchal Blessing, a Gift and a Guide," *Instructor*, Dec. 1960, p. 421.

14. Elmo J. Bergeson, "The Patriarchal Blessing, a Gift and a Guide," *Instructor*, Dec. 1960, p. 421.

15. Carlos E. Asay, "Write Your Own Blessing," *New Era*, Oct. 1981, p. 4.

16. "No Hands, No Eyes—But No 'Handicaps,'" *Ensign*, July 1979, p. 13.

17. Elmo J. Bergeson, "The Patriarchal Blessing, a Gift and a Guide," *Instructor*, Dec. 1960, p. 421.

18. "Being Patriarch Is a Humbling Call," *Church News*, 30 Nov. 1974, p. 10.

19. LeGrand Richards, "Patriarchal Blessings, *New Era*, Feb. 1977, p. 6.

20. Quoting Dallin H. Oaks, "Resurrection," *Ensign*, May 2000, p.15.

21. "Priesthood Restored," *Ensign*, Apr. 2004, p. 27.

# CHAPTER 7

## Understanding Your Blessing

Let's pretend you are in a car driving around to enjoy the scenery. After a while, you're not sure where you are. You pull over, parking in the scented coolness of welcome shade. You open the glove box, pulling out fast-food napkins, looking for a map.

If you have your patriarchal blessing, go get it. This is like pulling the map out of the glove box. You want to figure out where you are going.

However, many of us are puzzled by our blessings. Sometimes we question our own potential. Other times, contents within the blessing confuse us. We feel like we don't know where we're going, even though the map is in our hands.

On your imaginary trip, assume you now have the map open. You turn it every direction. If you could just figure out the map, you could use it. But you find it is sideways, then upside down. For it to help you, you know you must look at the map from the same viewpoint as the mapmaker.

Unfold your patriarchal blessing now. How could you figuratively read it sideways or upside down? Instead, how can you look at this map from the viewpoint of the Mapmaker?

Try this—read your blessing through, watching for every good quality you have. You want to see yourself as our Heavenly Father sees you. The "you" that Father sees is the real you. Since every good quality you have comes from God, these are divine qualities. Your good qualities, then, prove your divine nature. When you see your divine nature, you begin to see yourself as God sees you. This is the first step to understanding your blessing. It is like turning the map right side up.

From this starting point, our blessings, like the maps they are, show us the direction we need to go. We can turn our lives onto the road named "Doing What We Came To Do." In other words, understanding who we are leads to understanding what we can do. Who we are and our missions in life are inseparable.

The more we understand our blessings, the more we can use them in our lives. We want to get past the roadblocks of misunderstanding, misconception, and misinterpretation. These can lead to mistakes. Let us, then, consider some difficulties we experience in understanding our blessings.

# DIFFICULTY FROM MISUNDERSTANDING

How does misunderstanding our blessings get us into trouble? According to one mother, her daughter justified marrying outside the temple because her blessing stated that she would be "sealed" rather than "married" in the temple. Within weeks she was miserable, and within months she was divorced. Her life since has been anguished. (G.E.) Of course, the promised blessing may still some day be hers, but her decision to elope was based on misunderstanding.

The point of her story is twofold. First, we need to understand the language of the Lord. In this example, "married," in a technical sense, is a worldly term; in the Lord's eyes when we are joined in matrimony we are "sealed." If this bride had understood the Lord's perspective of marriage, perhaps she would have chosen differently. Second, we need to be careful so we don't misinterpret and twist our blessings to rationalize unwise decisions. The mother said the girl used the wording as an excuse for doing what she wanted to do. Her story emphasizes the importance of understanding our blessings in order to use them for our good.

Sometimes misconception leads to doubt. A student received his patriarchal blessing before going away to college. In talking to the patriarch beforehand, he failed to mention his strong desire to be an actor. Instead, he told him a "much more practical and less starry-eyed" story that he was going to be a teacher of theatre arts and English. He said:

*I had determined that the Lord knew of my true ambition. Surely He would reveal this to the patriarch after he placed his hands on my head and began giving me my blessing.*

*My testimony of patriarchal blessings was shaken when the patriarch pronounced over my head that I would become a teacher which is a "noble profession." My testimony of the validity of such blessings further eroded years later when a close friend shared portions of his blessing with me.*

The friend shared common theater experiences, interests, and ambitions. His blessing, given by the same patriarch, also indicated he would be a teacher, a "noble profession." But the first man went into university film production, and the second became a writer for Church films.

After years of divergent paths, the two are now setting up a partnership.

*We are finding it difficult if not impossible to develop a script for a motion picture that will simply entertain. We are finding that any project on which we collaborate must enlighten, enrich, and enhance life; it must, in short, teach.*

*We now know it was no cruel coincidence that our patriarchal blessings share the same phrase. We have discovered that our professional careers share a similar destiny. (L.T.)*

Misinterpretation can also make us think we have lost a blessing. An older woman said that her blessing told her she would be an inspiration to young women. At thirty she went through a messy divorce because she had been physically abused. She thought, "There goes that. They never use divorcees to teach in Young Women."

She moved to Arizona at the time when the Equal Rights Amendment was passing in states across the country. Arizona was the crucial turning-point state. She believed that the amendment was wrong and was intended to break up families. She helped organize a

Stop ERA movement, gathered 35,000 signatures, and went to the legislature. The amendment was defeated.

"I always thought the phrase in my patriarchal blessing meant I would be in the Young Women organization," she said. "But to stop ERA was more important. I affected a lot more young women." (C.R.#2)

An Institute instructor said that often promises are given "in generalities. When the time [for fulfillment] comes, then we understand the specific meaning." (W.E.)

# DISAPPOINTMENT—
# TOO SHORT

Perhaps the most common complaint about a patriarchal blessing is: "It's too short." One woman's comment is typical. "My blessing is very, very short. I received it when I was fourteen. I was then, and for many years remained, very disappointed." (S.C.)

Her perception of the brevity caused another problem. "The blessing was very impersonal. I always felt there was nothing special that Heavenly Father wanted to say to me. I interpreted this as meaning I was not special." (S.C.)

How sad for one of God's beloved daughters to feel this way for years. The real problem was not the length of the blessing but the length of her understanding, which did come abundantly, later. In contrast, another woman said, "I received my patriarchal blessing at age thirteen, and was impressed by it even though it was very short." (B.C.N.)

Actually, length of blessing has no relationship to the "specialness" of the person who receives it. President Heber J. Grant acknowledged that he received "a little blessing that would perhaps be about one third of a typewritten page." Yet, in his later years, he firmly stated, "That blessing foretold my life to the present moment."[1]

A grandmother felt for many years that her blessing was too short and was about to ask if she could have another one. Her new husband asked if he could look at it first. His insight helped her understand her blessing, and she was satisfied.

# DISAPPOINTMENT— CONFUSING

If brevity can cause problems in understanding a patriarchal blessing, so can verbiage. One woman commented, "My blessing bothered me for years because the ideas are all run together. It confused me. I couldn't tell where one idea stopped and another started. I couldn't tell which ideas were supposed to be related. Several sentences are over a hundred words long." (J.T.#1)

She shared how she sorted through the wordiness to gain understanding. "Finally, a handout at a lesson in church helped me. It was a blank page with four columns: counsel, gifts, warnings, and promises. As I filled in the page with phrases from my blessing, for the first time I saw and relished them as separate blessings each contributing to the whole."

Elder John A. Widtsoe, however, made another suggestion. He said, "Attention should be fixed upon the one great meaning of the blessing rather than upon particular statements."[2] His perspective helps us look past the details that confuse us to focus on the overall eternal journey.

In a similar way, a college student said, "When I got my patriarchal blessing, it was a very powerful, spiritual experience for me. Even though my blessing may be confusing or difficult to understand, I have a testimony that it is inspired. This helps me." (K.C.D.)

Sometimes an individual "can't understand all that's in it. Maybe it's well that he can't," said Joseph Fielding Smith.[3] Nonetheless, if we are confused, and "there seem to be things we do not understand, through continued faith, the time will come when the interpretation will be given us."[3] His promise as a Patriarch to the Church provides hope. After all, since God gave us the blessing, surely He wants us to understand it.

However, we rarely understand it all at once but are given understanding "line upon line, precept upon precept" according to our diligence and need. With faith and patience in the Lord, He will unfold the best timing for us to understand a certain phrase or promise.

We need to remember, too, that along the way our interpretation may not be the same as the Lord's. A young woman received a patriarchal blessing that promised her health when she would do what is right. She went on a mission but was sent home with encephalitis. This confused her because surely going on a mission was right. Finally she went back to the patriarch who gave the blessing. He asked her what she had been doing before she got sick. She had taught and prepared a sister for baptism who previously had gone through several sets of missionaries. The patriarch responded, "That was your mission. You made a covenant in the preexistence to help her. Your mission was over." (F.H.)

# DISAPPOINTMENT— TOO VAGUE

Like the woman who felt her blessing was impersonal because it was so short, many are disappointed because their blessings are vague. One person commented, "I kept thinking my blessing could be anybody's." (K.O.) As she matured, she saw its uniqueness.

We think, "If only my blessing was more specific, I could understand it," as though this would remove all obstacles. Even a blessing that is pointedly specific can create problems. At thirteen, a boy named Jay was told in his patriarchal blessing that "the first time he met the woman who was to be his wife he would know that she was the one."[5] A few years later, while he was a dinner guest at a home, the doorbell rang. When a young woman entered and stood in the shadow, he said to himself, "That's my wife." He immediately tried to win her love. She had no such inspiration and didn't like it. So his specific promise created problems.

Perhaps blessings are purposely vague. A story from Matthew Cowley illustrates an important reason why. When he was an Apostle, he read his parents' journals telling of building a little home in Wyoming. At stake conference, after its completion, they asked the visiting General Authority to dedicate it for them. Both journals recorded the same prayer.

*In that prayer Brother [Moses] Thatcher said, "Heavenly*

*Father, may a prophet, seer, and revelator be born under this roof." ... We lived there long enough for me to be born. I am glad I never read that before I was called to this position.*[6]

What if, instead of being tucked away in private journals and in the hearts of parents, the prophecy had been openly stated in Elder Cowley's patriarchal blessing? He would have carried that knowledge as a burden from his early years. Instead, he was glad he "never read that" before he was called.

We can understand Elder Cowley's feelings. Indeed, one father shared how his son was "scared off" by his patriarchal blessing. Not feeling he could measure up to the expectations, he purposely choose the opposite direction. (C.G.)

Making a transfer to our own lives, we can understand—even appreciate—why our blessings sometimes seem vague. Many things in our future, for good or temporary ill, we would rather not hear about ahead of time. These things we would rather face when we must and when the Spirit will strengthen us. Sometimes, though, we hear people make comments such as, "My blessing doesn't say anything about my [divorce, accident, or other adversity]," implying they wish it had.

Let's make an analogy. If you know that flight 1360 to St. Louis will crash, will you get on the airplane? What if, instead, your blessing says someday you will be in a plane crash? Since this is avoidable, you decide never to fly. What blessings—of places seen, relatives visited, special occasions enjoyed, time saved, and experience gained—will you lose? Your choices are stymied. You act from fear rather than faith and courage. Knowing ahead of adversity may block your enjoyment of life and impede your progress. Obviously, this is not the intent of a blessing. We can be grateful for those things in our blessings that are vague for our own good.

On the other hand, we may believe that wording in our blessing is vague when the opposite is true. One woman's blessing referred to her "associates" in life. "I thought it an odd word," she said, "because it was generic. Why didn't it say 'friends?'" A couple of years after joining an association, "it suddenly dawned on me that the word was precise," she said. "With that realization, a flood of new insight rushed into my mind as to what Heavenly Father wanted me to accomplish." (J.T.#1)

Perhaps there is a third reason for a frustratingly vague blessing. Our Father is a master teacher who allows us to use principles of agency and self-discovery to grow. A book on creative thinking told of a Greek oracle who was "intentionally ambiguous," forcing his listeners "to go beyond the first right answer… [and] to consult the wisdom of their own intuition, and consider alternatives." [7]

The book continued:

> General George S. Patton … said, "If you tell people where to go, but not how to get there, you'll be amazed at the results." He knew that posing a problem in an ambiguous way would give more freedom to the imaginations of the people who were working on the problem. [8]

Applying this concept, we can reword a scripture so it reads: "Wonder not, but hearken unto the words of the Lord, and ask the Father in the name of Jesus for what things soever ye shall stand in need. Doubt not, but be believing, and … work out your own [patriarchal blessing] with fear and trembling before him." (Moro. 9:27.)

Viewed in this way, grappling with vagueness and ambiguity in our blessings helps us to see more possibilities and to grow. One sister shared her struggle to understand her generic blessing:

> I have always felt a tug of disappointment about my patriarchal blessing because it was vague—at least other people seemed to have specific promises and promptings in areas of genealogy, or missionary work, or something! Mine didn't. Years later I finally took it to my bishop and asked if I couldn't please have more—since it was also short. My wise bishop quietly read it and looked up at me. The tears ran down his face, and he told me that I did not need specific instruction—I was a chosen daughter who would always use my free agency to bless those around me.

She added her experience since gaining this insight:

> I still at times find it frustrating—but I go to the Lord in prayer and I am given the next step or two to take. Perhaps my

*blessing is more than a blessing—it's a challenge to design my own destiny through my Heavenly Father. Had my blessing been more detailed, I might not have sought my Father in prayer so often for guidance." (M.R.)*

One divorced brother stated, "My blessing, which was given almost forty years ago, was a great disappointment." His reason? Most of the promises were "veiled or hidden in phrases that referred to the 'desires of my heart' or 'my choices.'" He added:

*In the past few years I have been forced to look at the true promises of my blessing. I am only now beginning to see that what the Lord wanted me to do was set my own goals based upon the righteous desires of my heart and work and strive for their accomplishment. He knew that had he given me specific promises, I would have sat around waiting for them to happen instead of actively pursuing their fulfillment. As I look at my blessing now, I can insert my goals in the place of the vague parts and then keep my priorities straight by following the counsel and heeding the warnings. The counsel and warnings make "prophetic sense" in the context of my new goals. (K.N.#2)*

A middle-aged man also struggled for years with his blessing. He wrote, "I was bothered to the point that I discussed it with my bishop and stake president." He received a recommend to go to his current stake patriarch. He continued:

*The patriarch read my blessing and asked me what bothered me about it. I told him that it was not specific; it was not detailed and was too short, and that I always wondered if the patriarch who gave me the blessing was too old when he gave it. He then proceeded to break the blessing down into small bits and pieces and explained as he went through every word and line. As he explained these things to me a great feeling of peacefulness came over me and I began to more fully understand for the first time....*

*He concluded, "There is no need for another blessing to be given, for the one you have is one of the very best."*

*The main point of clarification was that the blessing, in its simplicity, was stating that the Lord was allowing me to "write my own ticket by my faithfulness and obedience." Inherent in this was great responsibility, but whatever opportunities were placed before me, I realized the Lord had given me ample gifts and talents to exercise in his service. That service has brought me great joy.*

*From that day forward I have read my blessing often and received much comfort. I have also tried to write a "ticket" that is pleasing to the Lord. (A.I.E.)*

From his own experience, Brigham Young would have agreed with this insight. He and one or two others asked the first patriarch for a patriarchal blessing. President Young related:

*Father Smith ... said to us, "Sit down, and write every good thing you can think of in heaven and on earth, and I will sign my name to them, and they will be your patriarchal blessings. If you only live for them, they shall all come upon you, and more." Live for the blessings you desire, and you will obtain them, if you do not suffer selfishness, pride, or the least alienation from the path of true virtue and holiness to creep into your hearts.[9]*

As a young missionary, Elder Carlos E. Asay had once thanked Elder Alma Sonne for a beautiful setting-apart blessing. Elder Sonne had replied, "'Elder Asay, I had the power and right to say what I said, but remember, you will write your own blessing by the way you live and serve.' Then he added, 'Go and write the best blessing that has ever been written.'"[10] The concept is true with our patriarchal blessings. Elder Asay's life was greatly impacted by Elder Sonne's words—"write your own blessing by the way you live and serve."

President Lorenzo Snow stated, "Be as great as you want to be.... You will all be great someday, as great as you want to be."[11] Perhaps the problem is not a vague blessing but a vague idea of what we want to be. Perhaps the challenge is wanting to be as great as God knows we can be.

# DIFFICULTY—IDENTICAL

In a rare case, a man in his fifties who "never felt right" about his blessing, even when receiving it, went to his stake president. Except for gender-specific words, he and his wife had received identical blessings from the same patriarch. When the stake president opened the door for his appointment, the patriarch walked out. The stake president had discovered that the patriarch was giving the same memorized blessing to everyone. The request for another blessing was granted without any discussion. (C.G.)

In another rare case, a woman struggled for nearly twenty years to use her blessing as a guide in her life. At seventeen she had fasted and prayed to "receive the blessing the Lord had intended for me." She was shocked at girls' camp when Peggy [not her real name] claimed the scribe told her, after getting her blessing, that it was "almost identical" to all the blessings given in recent months. Peggy had then recited what sounded like her own blessing. "I told her that we just must have needed similar counsel and to forget it." That night "I prayed to know that I had my correct blessing. The reassurance I sought never came."

She went to BYU where she continued to pray about it but "never really felt that sweet peace of confirmation." Over the years she kept rereading it. "I felt nothing. Then I would tuck it away and figure that there must be something wrong with me."

At the end of an interview with her stake president one day when she was thirty-six, he asked if there was anything she wanted to discuss. She surprised herself by saying, "Yes, as a matter fact, there is."

The stake president's first inclination was to tell her that only one blessing is ever given. However, he opened up the handbook and found there may be occasions when a second blessing is appropriate. He then counseled with her bishop and the stake patriarch. Tears of joy ran down her cheeks when she was told she could receive a new blessing. "Now I love my patriarchal blessing," she said. "I know this blessing was tailor made for me" (T.B.)

Church procedure is in place today to prevent the situation these two experienced years ago. Each patriarch is accountable directly to his stake president who interviews him periodically and reviews the patriarch's book of recently given blessings. In general conference, Elder Boyd K. Packer recommended this be done twice a year and stated, "The periodic reading of blessings must not be neglected by the stake president."[12]

When given under proper inspiration, patriarchal blessings, like fingerprints, will be individual.

# DIFFICULTY—UNBELIEVABLE

Some of us find our blessings hard to believe. One woman said simply, "It's too good." (K.T.#5) Another said that when she received hers, she "didn't believe a word" of it. It kept telling her that she had many talents, but she couldn't see any in herself. In time, she began recognizing the talents it talked about. As she began seeing herself as God sees her, her belief in her blessing grew. (K.O.)

A woman in her fifties had "unbelievable" promises. Although they are not fulfilled, she maintains faith in them, saying simply, "I don't worry about them." (J.E.L.)

Indeed, faith eases the wait for blessings. The father of three young children said, "I began to doubt—instead of letting it unfold." Since then, as his personal prophecies have unfolded, his faith in those yet to come has grown. (T.T.#2)

In fact, one grandmother, over time, had seen "unbelievable" promises come to pass. "I didn't think they would be fulfilled," she said, "because I didn't feel worthy." (K.K.#2) When we doubt the Lord and don't believe His blessings, we might consider why. Then we can work to remove the roadblock to faith.

Some things may seem unbelievable for another reason. A woman said, "My mother's blessing said she was born of goodly parents and told her to counsel with them because no one loved and cared for her like they did. In actuality they were manipulative, severely abusive parents and as my mother puts it, 'Wouldn't care if I dropped dead and turned to dust on the spot.'

"When I asked her how she'd come to terms with such a glaring discrepancy, she said she hadn't really. 'I've always had trouble understanding that,' she said. Apparently her faith in the gospel isn't contingent on her blessing." (K.S.) This shows us that regardless of what we can't believe in our blessings, we can go forward until understanding comes. Hopefully the mother had faith in the rest of her blessing. Someday she will understand the why behind the phrase that doesn't make sense.

Let us consider this insight. "My husband agonized over his. You have to have faith. You need the full perspective. They are not always interpreted as expected." (T.D.) These are keys to answer our questions of believability.

# DISAPPOINTMENT— OMISSIONS

A patriarch counseled, "Don't be disappointed if something you wanted wasn't in your blessing. Be happy with what is there." One mother was devastated when her son's blessing made no mention of wife or children. Yet, today he has a lovely wife and a large family. Heavenly Father has more blessings to give us than we can name. Just because one is not specifically listed, the patriarch emphasized, "doesn't mean you won't enjoy it." (H.A.K.)

Things not said can cause the problem a young sister missionary faced. "On my mission I felt really bad for a while," she said, "because my companions would tell me how their blessings talked about their missions. I'd go and look at mine and couldn't find anything related to going on a mission. I'd feel bad like maybe I wasn't supposed to go. I believe it was something I didn't have to do, but it was a good choice. I'm forever grateful that I went. It doesn't bother me now that my blessing doesn't say anything about it." (K.C.D.)

A teenage girl sobbed because her blessing made no mention of a family. Bone cancer racked her frail body. But her blessing promised her eternal life. Her patriarch comforted her, explaining that she could not receive the great gift of eternal life without a family. Understanding eased her pain. (H.A.K.)

Many years ago, another patriarch wrestled for an answer as people came to him disappointed over omissions in their blessings.

He wrote:

> *Often I petitioned my Heavenly Father about it. One night I awakened and was unable to go back to sleep.... It came to me that a patriarchal blessing was given as an aid and a guide, that the Lord never intended to give a person a complete outline of his life nor that nothing but that which was mentioned would ever happen to him. I learned that one should pursue every Gospel principle, that he might be in condition for the Lord to give him added blessings and talents.*[13]

A Young Women leader, speaking of omissions of temple marriage or children for example, put it this way. "We can follow these gospel teachings on our own, without specific personal direction."[14]

# DISAPPOINTMENT— UNFULFILLED PROMISES

Some people complain that a promised blessing has not materialized. "There are only two reasons for this," one patriarch said. "Either the person is not worthy, or it is not time for it." Also, we can fail to recognize fulfillment. This happens because blessings are "sometimes realized in different ways from what we expect." [15] The "time for it" refers, of course, to the Lord's timetable, not our own. For some, like the girl with cancer, the time is the next life. As one older sister said, "I believe that some of my blessings might not come until my after-life, but I can live with that." (I.H.D.)

With faith, we, like this woman, can live with not receiving some blessings until later. The face-in-the-mirror question is: how will we feel if the reason for not receiving a blessing is unworthiness?

Sometimes we stretch the definition of "unworthiness." One woman said, "I didn't think they would be fulfilled because I didn't feel worthy. I have sins of omission because I tend to be lazy. I have been more blessed than I bless others." (K.K.#2) Yet, she was seeing blessings fulfilled.

Another woman struggled, too. "After a heart-wrenching divorce, I found it hard to reconcile myself to unfulfilled promises in my patriarchal blessing. As the years went on I learned to focus on the promises that had been fulfilled and the ones that could yet be. I continue to receive great motivation, comfort, and inspiration from my blessing, and my faith continually grows in regard to the phrases I don't understand. I could so easily have put it aside and never looked at it again. I'm so grateful I didn't do that." (E.J.) She chose to see "unfulfilled promises" as phrases she didn't understand and did all she could to be worthy.

We can look forward to fruition as the woman who said, "My patriarchal blessing makes a promise I haven't obtained yet, but I still have hope." (F.Z.) All patriarchal blessings are dependent on our faithfulness. If we do all we can to live for them, the so-called "unfulfilled" blessings will be received. In the end, therefore, we may fail fulfillment by choice.

Some have asked in anguish, "Is it too late? Have I lost the blessing while I was [inactive, errant, or whatever applies]?" This question cannot be answered with a blanket response. However, one patriarch stated, "We postpone the blessings. They go through the millennium and beyond. We might have forfeited them for the near term and for a time. We can forfeit them eternally if we continue [in the wrong path]. Once we have a blessing and a promise from the Lord, He holds the door open. We should do the best we can to gain the blessing. We can put ourselves in suspension with the foolish things we do." (H.I.)

Careful reading of the blessing may provide peace. Heavenly Father who gave the promises also knew the spirits He gave them to, including the trials they would face. Someone has defined repentance not as a second chance but as the "first chance over again."

Elder Robert L. Simpson made this encouraging statement: "Those of you who sit reluctantly in the wings, find your patriarchal blessing, dust it off, and read it again; contemplate deeply the Lord's personal message given to you alone.... There is yet time. It's never too late to pick up the pieces." [16] A woman who had been inactive twelve years got her blessing out and discovered it fit her life and her needs. (M.B.G.)

Even a faithful person may wait and worry about unfulfilled promises. By age 23, President Heber J. Grant was disturbed about an unfulfilled promise in his blessing that he would be called to the ministry in his youth. He hadn't been called as a missionary. He felt concern about his status and about the Church. Maybe the patriarch wasn't inspired. He grew confused even though he knew the Church was true. Why was he doubting? He could not find peace. One day as he was walking in Salt Lake City, negative thoughts tormented him again. He "stopped right there on the sidewalk and spoke out loud,... 'Mr. Devil, shut up. I don't care if every patriarch in the Church has made a mistake in a blessing, and told a lie, I believe with all my heart and soul that the gospel is true and I will not allow my faith to be upset.'" He was never tormented again, and he was shortly called as a stake president. The promise was fulfilled again at age 25 when he was ordained an Apostle.[17]

President Spencer W. Kimball also experienced frustration. His patriarchal blessing promised a mission to the Lamanite people. As a young man he was called in 1914 to the Swiss-German Mission where there were no Indians. Then war erupted, so he was sent to the Central States Mission where there were Indians. But in two years, he did not see an Indian. "I wondered, 'Can I have failed, or did the patriarch err,' and now, forty-two years after the promise,... my blessing was fulfilled."[18]

Forty-two years is a long time to wait but a "small moment" to God. Elder John A. Widtsoe said, "There must be no quibbling about the time or place when the promises should be fulfilled or about the man who gave it..., and its fulfillment will be in His hands."[19] On the other hand, disbelief and discouragement can cause us to lose our blessings. Paul V. Johnson, a Church Educational System administrator, spoke on Satan's attempts to encourage us to break our covenants.

> One of Satan's subtle messages is that the promised blessings won't actually come. We can't control the timing of the blessings, but they will come. Part of the test is to see if we will remain strong when the promises haven't been fulfilled yet. I wonder how many members of the church have wavered and broken their covenants because the promised blessings weren't on the time line they had envisioned?"[20]

Being worthy is one matter. Helping the promises along to fruition is another. As one woman said, "We can't just read them and say, 'Oh, that will happen someday.'" (C.R.#2) We cannot expect the blessings to be fulfilled without any effort on our part.

As Elder Antoine R. Ivins said, "The blessings that are promised to us throughout the Church are dependent upon our efforts to help them come to pass. I never have felt that a patriarchal blessing was a prediction as to what must come to pass, but what might come to pass if we would help conditions so that those things could be realized." [21]

Ultimately, then, the fulfillment of our blessings is dependent upon us, for we can count on the Lord to keep his promises. As one man put it, "Sometimes people think their blessings are not fulfilled. They need to remember two things: (1) The Lord never lies. (2) The blessings are inspired even though we don't see it now. The Lord doesn't allow his servants the patriarchs to lie when they are serving.... There are people who have patriarchal blessings who have yet to have enough faith that it will be so. Go ask and have that witness that it will be so." (R.I.#1)

If we believe the promises, stay worthy, and work for them, they will be fulfilled. President Kimball taught that a patriarchal blessing is a "conditional prophecy" with "no guarantee that the blessings will be fulfilled unless the individual subscribes to the program, but, I bear my testimony to you that none of the blessings he pronounces will fail if the participant of the blessing fully subscribes." [22] That is the testimony of a prophet.

# DISAPPOINTMENT— ALL FULFILLED

Some people are disappointed because they believe the promises in their blessings are all fulfilled and there is nothing left to look forward to. According to patriarchs, such disappointment is based on misconception. As you go through life, one said, "your perspectives and your needs are different. Your blessing has something for all your life. Don't ever say your blessing doesn't have much value any more. I think Heavenly Father would be offended." Instead, he recommended reading your blessing often for new insights. (H.A.K.)

Another said, "A young mother felt her blessing was finished. I told her it is more than words. It's feelings. The Savior fed 5,000 with five loaves and two fishes. He said that was enough. The disciples said it was not. The Savior said to eat until you are full. Eat all you want. Then bring back what is left. Twelve baskets came back. We cannot consume all the gospel has. The next day there is more. There is more to your blessing than meets the eye." (R.V.)

# UNDERSTANDING— THROUGH EXPERIENCE

The blessing of one multi-talented young mother specified her most important role in life. Yet, it took perspective brought by experience before she understood that her blessing was telling her to put family first.

*For many years, because of the brevity and simplicity of my blessing, the significance of it escaped me. Then when I was 35 years old—I began to understand.*

*All my life I have performed, held leadership positions, opened businesses, traveled, etc. I have been blessed with talents and abilities, more than I deserve. And yet, I have always put family first—even when I would rather they be last!*

*I realized that the Lord knew me far better than I knew myself. He also has known me for longer than I have been "earthly aware" of myself. He knew the events of my life, what I would achieve and become involved in.*

*So knowing—he helped me concentrate in the one way that he could. Knowing this, at the very time of my life when I would have the most opportunities, then I would understand that "No other success can compensate for failure in the home." By remembering this and my calling as a mother, I would be able to sail clearly through the storms of life. (S.C.)*

Sometimes a specific experience will illuminate a specific promise given in a blessing. An older sister wrote of such an experience.

*At the time I received my blessing the promise that impressed me the most was that if I should share whatever came into my possession with those less fortunate or those in need, I would always be provided for and never want for the necessities of life. When my husband and I were serving a mission in Liverpool, England,... we lived just around the corner from the church. We invited the bishopric and members of the ward who would be attending the conference to come to our flat for lunch. We also invited the two sisters serving in our zone who, unknown to us, invited all the elders to come.*

*I had filled the biggest pot we had, which held about six quarts, and made a beef stew, bought three sticks of French bread, and felt prepared. After the morning session of conference we hurried home to warm up the stew, and people started coming and coming and kept coming. Our sparsely furnished living room was larger than most, but it was full. Most people were sitting on the floor. We filled every cup, every bowl and plate we had, serving over thirty people, and when we had given everyone all they wanted, we had one small cup of stew left. We felt the meal had been provided by the Lord that day."* (B.C.N.)

As we see a literal fulfillment of a simple promise, as she did, we gain clearer understanding and faith that all the other blessings will also unfold.

Sometimes our blessings will open up understanding to seemingly unrelated issues. One woman wrote:

*I married a new convert whose background was tremendously different from my own. Over the years when he didn't choose temple blessings, I struggled to accept our differences. I sometimes agonized over my decision to marry him—although I had felt great peace about it at the time.*

During those years she frequently puzzled over a sentence in her patriarchal blessing. She would do vicarious work for her loved ones, it told her, but thousands of names were already done. She said:

*I will never forget the day I received my answer. I was simply walking across the kitchen, after having read this part of my blessing again, when suddenly a thought came into my mind that could not be from me. I suddenly knew that sentence refers to my husband's family who have passed on—most of whom have not had their temple work done. Along with the thought came that warm, overwhelming feeling that I know is the Holy Ghost, and tears slid down my cheeks....*

*The implications of that personal revelation just keep coming to me, and I am so grateful for my patriarchal blessing. If my husband's family are my loved ones, then my marriage to him was foreknown. I must have known those people and loved them before I came here, and they saw me as part of their family.*

*I have renewed hope that my husband will seek temple blessings and that I will eventually be sealed to him. I am reassured that my marriage, no matter how challenging it has been, was right, that I wasn't spiritually weak or impatient or misled when I married someone who wasn't ready to go to the temple. Such a weight off my shoulders, such a joy to my soul!* (E. J.)

# UNDERSTANDING— THROUGH SPECIFIC SUGGESTIONS

Instead of waiting for life to give us perspective, we can do some simple things to increase understanding of our blessings. One mother wrote simply, "I read my blessing often." (L.P.) Her point is so obvious that we overlook it—we must read our blessings if we ever hope to understand them. A senior missionary added a step. "To understand your blessing, it's important to read it and read it and look at what's going on in your life at the time. Some things become apparent as different things happen in your life." (N.M.)

We start understanding our blessings, then, by getting them out of the drawer, or, if necessary, by searching to find them.

The mother added, "My blessing is personal scripture to me." (L.P.) President Benson popularized the term "personal scripture." To see our patriarchal blessings as personal scripture, we must first recognize that God has revealed and given this blessing to us alone. This is the foundation on which understanding must be based.

In addition to reading our blessings regularly, there are specific ways we can work to increase our understanding of them. One brother urged, "To understand more—go to the scriptures or to *Mormon Doctrine.*" As an older single man, he was concerned because "My blessing does not state I will have a temple marriage." However, by looking up a phrase used in his blessing, he discovered that its meaning included a temple marriage. A little study had revealed the promised blessing that he sought.

This same brother looked up the meaning of another unfamiliar phrase in his blessing, "fruits of the spirit." He found it by looking "in Galatians where it speaks of 'long suffering, patience, tolerance, etc.'" With this clear definition in the scriptures, he could understand his blessing. (K.C.#1) A computerized scripture program can aid this type of search.

Another brother researched the topic of calling and election. His personal study explained some things in his patriarchal blessing for him.

Similarly, one woman looked up "diligent" in a dictionary. She found the word meant "characterized by steady, earnest, and energetic application and effort; painstaking." The details of the definition gave her additional insight.

Another specific way to study and understand her blessing was discovered by a woman with fourteen children in a "yours, mine, and ours" situation. She wrote:

> A couple of years ago I met a young man who had done much research on chiasmus, a form of literary expression. In the scriptures and other inspired writings this is a common characteristic. He even went so far as to declare it to be the "Signature of God," a way of identifying truth revealed through

*the Holy Spirit. He suggested that patriarchal blessings could show this pattern.*

*I took some time and prayer and pondering to study my blessing in this context. As I worked my way through the words and phrases I found that the central message or focal point of my blessing referred to the promise that if I set as a goal in this life the sealing of all my loved ones to me, that the Lord would work with me and for me to accomplish this. (B.I.)*

Chiasmus is "a rhetorical pattern that matches elements in reverse order; that is, the first element parallels the last, the second element parallels the next-to-last, and so on."[23] Some say that as a literary devise chiastic patterns put the heart of a message in the center.

A sister passed along this suggestion for understanding our blessings. "While reading your blessing make a list of all of the blessings the Lord has promised you. Divide them into two columns. In the first column, put those blessings that are just given to you outright. In another column put those blessings that are predicated on your doing or learning a particular thing. I actually did do this, and it was very enlightening. The first column made me feel very grateful for all of the blessings I have. The second column gave me some food for thought and an idea of what I needed to be working on in my life to fully realize the blessings that the Lord has in store for me." (K.D.)

"A variation on this," wrote another sister, "is to make a column with the things the Lord has asked of you and then the blessings that go with obedience to those particular principles." (C.K.)

Of the many specific ways we can use to help us understand our blessings, most important is prayer, patience, and whisperings of personal revelation.

# UNDERSTANDING — THROUGH A LOVED ONE'S BLESSING

We are permitted to read the blessings of close family members, our spouse, our direct line ancestors, and descendants. We need permission of the owners if they are living.

Sometimes we gain understanding about ourselves through the patriarchal blessing of one of our family members. A wife said:

> When I read my husband's patriarchal blessing, the Spirit told me that it was a completion of my own. I received mine at age fifteen. It was full of good advice, but besides saying I would marry in the temple,... it gave no foretelling.... It never mentioned the things I love such as music or writing.
>
> I love my blessing and use it as scripture. I love my husband's for we are now one, and his blessing tells of the future and we will be together through it all. (K.T.#4)

A woman whose mother had died when she was five had read her mother's patriarchal blessing several times before.

> Last night ... I got to a part that promised her protection yet she died at twenty-seven. It confused me. I kept reading. The next paragraph sounded like it depended on her choice of a righteous mate and suddenly everything made sense. My dad is now in jail. I think my mom was taken from this earth to spare her of all that....
>
> What it really helped me to see was that the blessings that are given to us are contingent on our behavior. Possibly if she had made a different choice on who to marry she would have been protected.
>
> My blessing tells me some things that are contingent and it makes me look at those areas closer and look at the way I should go. Even though she may not have chosen the best person to marry, I don't know that was the wrong choice. Just because she died doesn't mean she wasn't protected. It could be true even though she was taken. Like Eve, she may have had to go through those things so the things meant to be could be. I know she is one of the great and noble spirits.
>
> ... I realize that she continues mothering. How many times I've felt her. The blessings are not just for this life and continue to be fulfilled even after death. (K.K.#1)

One widow related:

*This is not about my own blessing, but my deceased husband's. He died suddenly from a coronal aneurysm at the age of forty-one. It was a great shock to me, and I had difficulty understanding the "why" of the situation. After some months I discovered a copy of his patriarchal blessing which I studied intently looking for some sign that might have explained it all.*

*As I read and reread again and again, it was all there. The wording was such that he might have lived to 100 or died when he did. There was nothing undone, but everything to do. His mission was one of service to God's children in and out of the church. As an elementary teacher, his work with children was exceptional. Serving both a full-time mission and a stake mission, he carried the message of the gospel. As a counselor in three different bishoprics, beginning before we were even married, he filled his stewardship with compassion and effectiveness. As a father, he taught his children the principles of the gospel and was a good example to them.*

*... Surely, he had fulfilled his mission on this earth to the satisfaction of his Heavenly Father because a priesthood blessing which could have brought him back during the time of medical possibilities was accompanied by sufficient faith to do so. The fact that he died attests to the scripture in the Doctrine and Covenants that he was appointed unto death. (D&C 42:48.)*

*Sometimes our blessings offer understandings of life on this earth to others besides ourselves and more than life—death.* (C.H.E.)

Another family found the same kind of consolation after the mother was killed in a car accident on the way to a temple session. The family had a hard time adjusting to her death, and the children felt that her death was untimely. When the family read her patriarchal blessing, they came to understand that her time on earth was fulfilled. In turn, this understanding brought them peace and comfort. (S.P.)

A speaker at BYU mentioned that his father's blessing had

promised that he and his sons would help build the temple in Jackson County, Missouri. He said people asked "how in the world" this could be when the father was deceased. He felt their question missed the point. As one of the sons, he said, "I am only concerned about whether his sons will all be faithful enough to be there to join him." [24] Rather than seeing what some would call a sensational promise, he saw that his father's blessing held an additional one for him. His father's blessing enriched his own life.

Perhaps greater insight into ourselves is one reason why we can request blessings of direct line family members through Church archives. (See chapter 2 for details.)

# THE WAY TO UNDERSTANDING

A patriarchal blessing helps us understand ourselves. As we understand ourselves better, we understand our blessings better. It is circular. As we understand our blessings better, we can use them more effectively in our lives. As we use them more, we understand them and ourselves more, and the circle enlarges.

Nevertheless, while using our blessings as a map along the way, most of us have questions. Elder Hugh W. Pinnock in a seminar for patriarchs in 1985 counseled them, "Don't try to answer all the questions specifically" for people about their blessings. "Have them prayerfully consider and obtain personal revelation and get the answer from the Lord who gave it." (Letter from H.I. to author.) This agrees with a statement made by a former Apostle, John A. Widtsoe, "As the blessing was given through the inspiration of the Lord, so its meaning will be made clear by the same power." [25] We can come to understand our blessings through personal revelation.

"The Almighty giveth them understanding." (1 Ne. 4:6.) We are entitled to receive our own interpretation first hand.

# SOURCES

1. Heber J. Grant, comp. by G. Homer Durham, *Gospel Standards*, Salt Lake City: *Improvement Era*, 1943, p. 12.

2. John A. Widtsoe, *Evidences and Reconciliations*, Salt Lake City: Bookcraft, 1943, p. 76.

3. Joseph Fielding Smith, "Patriarchal Blessings," Charge to Religious Educators, Salt Lake City: Church of Jesus Christ of Latter-day Saints, 1981, p. 122.

4. Eldred G. Smith, "What Is a Patriarchal Blessing?" *Instructor*, Feb. 1962, p. 43.

5. Matthew Cowley, *Matthew Cowley Speaks*, Salt Lake City: Deseret Book Co., 1954, p. 416.

6. Matthew Cowley, *Matthew Cowley Speaks*, Salt Lake City: Deseret Book Co., 1954, p. 425.

7. Roger Von Oech, *A Whack on the Side of the Head: How to Unlock Your Mind For Innovation*, New York: Warner Books, 1983, pp. 79-80.

8. Ibid., p. 81.

9. Brigham Young, "Instructions to Missionaries," *Journal of Discourses*, vol. 8, p. 54.

10. Carlos E. Asay, "Write Your Own Blessing," *New Era*, Oct. 1981, p. 4.

11. Clyde J. Williams, comp., *Teachings of Lorenzo Snow*, Salt Lake City: Bookcraft, 1984, p. 2.

12. Boyd K. Packer, "The Stake Patriarch," *Ensign*, Nov. 2002, p. 44.

13. Elmo J. Bergeson, "The Patriarchal Blessing, a Gift and a Guide," *Instructor*, Dec. 1960, p. 420.

14. Julie B. Beck, "You Have a Noble Birthright," *Ensign*, May 2006, p. 107.

15. Eldred G. Smith, "What Is a Patriarchal Blessing?" *Instructor*, Feb. 1962, p. 43.

16. Robert L. Simpson, *Conference Report*, Oct. 1969, p. 11.

17. Sherrie Mills Johnson, "Heber J. Grant: A Prophet for Hard Times," *Ensign*, Jan. 2004, p. 59.

18. Spencer W. Kimball, *Conference Report*, Apr. 1947, p. 145.

19. John A. Widtsoe, *Evidences and Reconciliations*, Salt Lake City: Bookcraft, 1943, p. 76.

20. www.byui.edu/News/NewsReleases/johnson.html, 26 Nov. 2001.

21. Antoine R. Ivins, *Conference Report*, Oct. 1961, p. 28.

22. Edward L. Kimball, ed., *Teachings of Spencer W. Kimball*, Salt Lake City: Bookcraft, 1982, p. 504.

23. Allen J. Christenson, "Chiasmus in Mayan Texts," *Ensign*, Oct. 1988, p. 28.

24. Carl W. Buehner, *BYU Speeches*, 19 Oct. 1960, p. 4.

25. John A. Widtsoe, *Evidences and Reconciliations*, Bookcraft, 1943, p. 76.

# CHAPTER 8

*Using Your Blessing*

## PURPOSES

"A patriarchal blessing gives you ideals to live up to," a seminary student wrote. (C.C.A.) That's a good starting definition for the purpose of our blessings.

A Patriarch to the Church said, "If you can discover the keynote in your blessing, it will be an index to point the way of life for you, or the path that you should go to serve God." [1]

What is a keynote? A keynote is "the fundamental or central fact, idea, or mood." [2] In other words, look for a central idea in your blessing. This keynote, pointing the way for your life, is a major purpose of your blessing and may be tied to your mission in life.

There is another major purpose. Adam blessed his family because "he wanted to bring them into the presence of God." [3] The over-riding purpose for our blessings is the same. Our Father, who bestows the blessings, wants to bring us into His presence.

We need the atonement of our Savior to accomplish this. With "every patriarchal blessing," Elder Bruce R. McConkie said, "all was ordained ... to testify of his Son and center the faith of believing people in him and in [his] redemption." [4] We might read our blessings specifically looking for ways they testify of Christ. It is true that "the firmer our faith in Jesus Christ, the clearer our vision of ourselves and what we can ultimately achieve and become." [5]

We receive our blessings in faith. Then our blessings open our vision by giving our identity. This is like a key to the promises we inherit through our lineage. Remember we are "children of the prophets" and heirs of the covenant of Abraham. (See chapter 4.) Seeing this broadens our perspective and gives us an even clearer view of ourselves, here and now, and in eternity.

The purpose of our blessings is not to give us answers to every problem. This would infringe on agency. Speaking of patriarchal blessings as Patriarch to the Church, Eldred G. Smith, said:

> Do not wait until you are troubled and then go to the Lord through his holy servants. The Lord does not intend to solve our problems for us. He gives us special problems for our good, to teach us to make decisions because through making those decisions and through those trials we have the privilege of growing, and the Lord does not intend to take that privilege from us.[6]

We can, however, use guidance in our blessings to make decisions that lead us back to our Father. Once we understand the purpose of our blessings, we are ready to begin using them in our lives.

## USES

Our patriarchal blessings have many uses. Some metaphoric descriptions show a few of these uses:

+ "A gift of the Lord.... A source of divine help in life's journey."[7]
+ "It is a guidepost; a white line down the middle of the road; a series of stakes around the mountain pass with reflector buttons in them so that whenever needed in the darkness and in the storm, they are available. The blessing can be reread like the reflectors that come up as the car approaches them on the turns."[8]
+ "Paragraphs from the book of your possibilities."[9]
+ "An eternal anchor for our soul."[10]
+ "Remember, your patriarchal blessing is your passport to peace in this life. It is a Liahona of light to guide you unerringly to your heavenly home."[11]
+ "A significant source of light."[12]

A few quotations show a sample of what a blessing can do:

+ "An inspired patriarchal blessing could light the way and lead the recipient on a path to fulfillment. It could lead him to become a new man and to have in his body a new heart."[13]

+ "To receive, and then consistently and prayerfully ponder one's patriarchal blessing can give helpful insight, particularly in an hour of need."[14]

+ "A patriarchal blessing gives us courage to live as we know we should live."[15]

In addition to a declaration of lineage, among the possible contents in a patriarchal blessings are the following:

+ guidance
+ answers to personal questions
+ encouragement
+ reassurance
+ commendation
+ blessings
+ cautions
+ warning
+ admonition
+ comfort
+ counsel
+ protection
+ personal strengths
+ statement of life mission
+ statement of fulfillment conditional upon faithfulness

Elder John A. Widtsoe summarized:

*Blessings are added as the Spirit may indicate, to meet our special requirements in life for our comfort, success, and strength. Our special needs may be pointed out; special gifts may be promised us; we may be blessed to overcome our weaknesses, to resist temptation, or to develop our powers, so that we may the more surely achieve the promised blessings. … A patriarchal blessing always confers promises upon us, becomes a warning against failure in life, and a means of guidance in attaining the blessings of the Lord."* [16]

# PERSONAL SCRIPTURE

The promises, warnings, and guidance Elder Widtsoe spoke of in our blessings sounds like the purpose of scriptures. In turn, President Ezra Taft Benson told us how to use our blessings. He said "Study it carefully and regard it as personal scripture to you—for that indeed is what it is.... [R]ead it regularly that you may know God's will for you." [17]

A mother passed on these suggestions for studying our blessings as scripture:

> When my daughter received her blessing, the patriarch suggested that she make several copies of it so that she could use it and still preserve the original. He also suggested that she put a copy of it in her scriptures so that she could read it often as part of her scripture study. He recommended, too, that she mark it and record her thoughts and feelings in the margins as she pondered and prayed about her blessing. (L.P.)

Listed for easy reference, the patriarch recommended to her:

+ Make several copies.
+ Put a copy in your scriptures.
+ Read it often as part of scripture study.
+ Mark it, recording thoughts and feelings in the margins.
+ Ponder and pray.

One missionary took the concept of personal scripture literally.

> As a missionary in Brazil, I was involved in a daily study of the scriptures.... I was engrossed in the power of the scriptures, but I wanted to find a way to apply them to me on a very personal level. This is when I decided to study the scriptures along with my own personal scripture, my patriarchal blessing. I bought a new notebook to use for my study session. For each idea or phrase in my blessing, I searched the scriptures for cross-references. When I found a scriptural passage I felt applied well, I recorded it in my notebook underneath the phrase from my blessing (highlighting the key words). I developed my own cross-referencing guide for my patriarchal blessing.

*I found that this form of study has really been valuable to me. Not only did I learn much as I prepared the notebook, I also have something to continue to study. The cross-referencing study not only helped me to learn more about the scriptures on a personal level, but also helped me to understand my patriarchal blessing much more. (C.V.C.)*

A woman said, "Tying it into the scriptures helps make the scriptures more relevant when I see the same admonitions and promises from the scriptures in my personal blessing, as well as helping me to understand parts of my blessing in new ways."

She explained her method for doing this. "When studying my blessing, I typed it up leaving big spaces between paragraphs and added scriptural footnotes. For example, my blessing talks about teaching so I looked up scriptures about teaching and made notations from relevant scriptures, adding that counsel and blessings. I started doing that when I first got my blessing and didn't really understand the gift of discernment." (C.K.)

Another woman suggested making a list of personal characteristics that are in your patriarchal blessing and then watch for them and underline them in your scripture reading. (G.E.) Put together, the two women's suggestions provide an expanded cross referencing system. This system will work well with the following ideas.

Some people reduce their blessings in a copy machine to scripture page size for convenience and laminate it to preserve it. Lamination also allows you to mark with a dry erase pen for temporary study. Some have also typed it in columnar form with "verse" numbers on each paragraph, giving the blessing the appearance of scripture. Running a glue stick along the inside edge will allow it to be permanently inserted into regular scriptures. These methods make our "personal scriptures" handy to give us personal guidance.

## GUIDING OUR LIVES

President Benson gave us a "why" and a "how" for using our patriarchal blessings.

*Jesus knows that His kingdom will triumph, and He wants you to triumph with it. He knows in advance every strategy the enemy will use against you and the kingdom. He knows your weaknesses and He knows your strengths. By personal revelation you may discover some of your strengths through a careful and prayerful study of your patriarchal blessing.*[18]

How many ways are there to use your patriarchal blessing? There must be as many ways as there are people for we are each unique. Here are some ways others use their blessings.

## STRENGTH

A bishop gained strength:

*Specific promises in my patriarchal blessing have given me faith, hope and confidence for facing the future, as I know the blessing is from the Lord. Areas of my life that cause concern have been strengthened because of the promises.*

*It has been a guide and source of strength in helping me govern my life and maintain a true perspective of the desires I have for the future as well as the present. (F.A.R.)*

Similarly, "Patriarchal blessings can comfort us in times of loss, be an anchor in dark days, and strengthen us as we make a daily effort to choose the right."[19]

## GOALS

A young single sister used her blessing to set goals.

*I use my patriarchal blessing as a way to help me set goals, for example going on a mission with my husband later in life. I am also preparing myself for a temple marriage with a returned missionary as stated in my blessing. (K.V.)*

In a similar way another young single sister said, "My patriarchal blessing has helped me make a lot of crucial decisions. I've set my goals and priorities in life, and I'm working hard to accomplish what Heavenly Father wants me to do."[20]

As a teenager, one Young Women leader was told her test scores showed she would not succeed in college. "But after I prayerfully studied my patriarchal blessing, I felt I should not abandon my lifelong goal." With the Lord's plan in her hand, she earned her degree.[21]

## COURAGE/ENCOURAGEMENT

A grandmother found courage. "We don't have to fear. It gives us a picture of where we are going," she said. (G.V.)

A middle-age man gained encouragement:

> The patriarch said among other things that the blessing was to be used as a guide throughout my life. I received it when I was twelve years old and have constantly referred back to it.... Whenever I feel discouraged I read my blessing, rededicate myself to the Lord's work, and I find answers to my other problems. (K.F.I.)

A young mother of six children used her patriarchal blessing to overcome discouragement in times of trial. After reading it, she felt renewed with the knowledge that she can cope. (K.M.)

Elder Jay E. Jensen told of discouragement weighing him down after dealing with numerous problems as a mission president. After four days of extensive meetings, he settled in his airplane seat brooding and heavy-hearted. He took out his scriptures. Inserting his name into the verses, he read, "Behold, you, Jay Jensen, have been entrusted with these things, ... and remember also the promises which were made to you, Jay Jensen [D&C 3:5]."

Elder Jensen commented:

> During those four days I had focused on nothing but problems. I had not stopped to consider one single promise.

> I had with me on the airplane that day a copy of my patriarchal blessing. I read it, noting several marvelous promises.

As he read it, his gloom lifted, and he returned to the scriptures to ponder other promises.[22] After focusing entirely on his problems, he found great encouragement in the promises.

## REASSURANCE

A teenage boy found reassurance. "My blessing was a great blessing to me. I was in a car accident shortly after I received it. I had promises… It gave me great peace of mind. I told my mom, 'I'll be all right.' My blessing was not fulfilled yet. I was fourteen." (C.R.#1)

## PEACE

A young adult found peace. She said, "I received my patriarchal blessing five years ago, and I have made the goal to read it once a week because of the personal guidance, comfort, peace and strength I gain from it. In every situation or disappointing time throughout life, I always find peace through reading my blessing. It always answers many questions and concerns I find during life." (O.N.)

One brother finds another kind of peace in his blessing. As a young man, he received his blessing without thinking about the foolish things he had done, but words in his blessing made him realize. "To think that the Lord was … willing to overlook and forgive the foolishness of youth … touched me very deeply. I have returned to read those words many times and have reflected that if he forgave me then, perhaps he will continue to forgive me and grant me the blessings of peace." [23]

## COMFORT

An older single sister found sustaining comfort through her blessing:

> My patriarchal blessing speaks at length about experiences I had in the preexistence in preparing me for earth life. When the world seems to come crashing in on me, I draw on this knowledge that I was aware of the circumstances I would be in and I was given specific, spiritual preparation for all I would encounter here. (K.K.I.)

A single man said he read his patriarchal blessing more frequently during holidays because it helps prevent "'comparing your situation with those around you, but instead focusing on our mission here on earth and Jesus Christ's Atonement for us.'" [24] That focus gave comfort, shoving loneliness aside.

Another man said, "I was told about my children. That was a pretty neat trick, I thought, since I in no way had plans for getting married at that point in time. I was told that I would need all the knowledge and wisdom that I have (or ever would have) to keep my children in the straight and narrow path. To many that might have been a scary thought; to me it was a great comfort." (V.B.H.)

"At times when I feel like I'm stumbling down the path of righteousness," a teenage girl said, "my patriarchal blessing can be such a comfort to me." [25]

## INSIGHT

We can gain insight. A teenager said, "I learned many things about myself that day." [26] She might have learned her talents, her purpose, or her potential, among other things. Sometimes the things learned are vitally important to our mortal or spiritual success, such as acknowledging a weakness we didn't know we had. Sometimes what we learn comes through the heart. "I felt unloved," one person said. "When I felt my Heavenly Father's love, I began to believe that maybe others could love me too." (H.T.)

## PERSPECTIVE

Eternal perspective can come. When Nikki, a girl with disabilities, received her patriarchal blessing, "she was told she had been given this special experience in mortality because of the greatness of her soul." [27] A Young Woman leader who received her blessing while young commented, "from that day onward I began to think more often in terms of eternity than popularity." [28]

Busy with daily life, a mother of six said her blessing helped her "to keep perspective. 'Now' is a small part of my life. It keeps me humbled. It helps keep my thoughts toward Heavenly Father and His plan for me." (D.I.)

## GUIDANCE

We can receive guidance. A single brother said, "My blessing gives guidance to me every time I read it. It puts my perspective back in order." (V.L.)

One woman said:

> *I feel particularly blessed as my grandfather gave me my patriarchal blessing.... When I need direction and comfort in my life I reread my blessing. The spirit of peace and guidance that comes says to me, "Dear granddaughter, this blessing is true, live up to its principles and you will always be guided and blessed." (I.H.D.)*

A young woman's patriarchal blessing told her what to look for in her husband. From this she said she recognized him. (M.T.) After pondering her blessing, another young woman admitted the young man she was dating didn't match the description of her husband given in it. This realization helped her break up with him. (J.T.#2)

Our blessings, like a compass, can point the direction for us to go. There are "things in our blessings for us in times when we are lost." (E.A.)

## SPECIFIC ANSWERS

A young adult received specific answers:

> *After coming back into the Church after inactivity, a friend suggested I get my patriarchal blessing. I had been involved with drugs and alcohol very heavily during the past two years. I had also been raped but because I was drunk thought it was my fault and thus I had been immoral in my mind. I had been working with my bishop and on my own to change my life. I read the Book of Mormon for the first time and had gained a very strong testimony of its truthfulness. I had some major fears because of the things I had been involved with:*
>
> *(1) Who would ever want me after I'd been immoral?*
>
> *(2) What if my children had birth defects because of me?*
>
> *(3) I couldn't remember most of what I had read in the Book of Mormon. How could I ever share it?*
>
> *(4) Did Heavenly Father really love and forgive me in spite of my sins?*
>
> *(5) Was it really possible for me to make it to the celestial kingdom, especially because of my past?*

*An amazing thing happened. All my questions were answered. I had prayed, cried and pleaded with the Lord to know the answers to these questions. I was told of His love for me. I was told of my husband to be and that my children would be strong and healthy. Also I was assured that as I studied I would come to understand and remember the scriptures. Last but not least I was told that if I was faithful I would, for real, be in the celestial kingdom. My whole life has been different, and 100% better since this great event in my life. (K.M.N.)*

A college freshman also wanted specific answers. "I had a list," he said, "personal things I wanted the Lord to reveal to me in my patriarchal blessing. Each day during the week leading up to receiving my blessing, I prayed often asking for the Lord to guide me. As I prayed I referred to my list.... I distinctly remember the strong spirit I felt as the Lord answered my fervent prayers and often times used similar wording as I had used on my list.... Each time I read my blessing I remember my list and my prayers and I once again realize that the Lord knows me, that he loves me, and that he speaks to me. I asked and I received." (C.V.C.)

## CHANGE

We can also use our patriarchal blessings to change our lives. While rereading his patriarchal blessing, "Robert realized that he had let his Heavenly Father down by neglecting the gospel in his life. Nudged by his conscience, he went to see his bishop."[29]

## PHYSICAL HEALTH

We can find hope for physical health. As a patriarch finished a blessing, the recipient and his wife began to sob. Afterward, the husband said, the patriarch asked "the reason for my tears. I told him that I had been diagnosed with cancer and that I only had two years to live and that the blessing he pronounced was almost too good to hope for. He assured me that it was the Lord's blessing and he was only a conduit." The man enjoyed many years, serving in numerous leadership positions.[30]

A pregnant woman in Brazil wept bitterly. Her father was on

the way to the hospital, dying. She had not prayed for some time. "In desperation I implored the Lord for forgiveness, and a voice whispered in my ear, 'Read your patriarchal blessing!' How could I think about my patriarchal blessing at a time like this? But the prompting continued, strongly urging me to read the blessing." She did so and "something amazing happened." She realized from promises there that her father would not die but would live to see her child grow. "My blessing was my answer that day."[31]

## EMOTIONAL HELP

We can find hope for emotional needs. "'In my darkest moments I was always somehow guided to my patriarchal blessing,'" a woman who had suffered childhood abuse wrote. "'Therein were words of hope and descriptions of a life filled with joy, love, an eternal family, and the gospel. Often I would plead with God to help me believe that those blessings could really come true for someone as pathetic as I felt. I literally clung to the blessings promised, with hope that I could be happy someday. My testimony grew as I saw the Lord fulfilling promised blessings in my life.'"[32]

## BENEFITS

A convert of fifteen years wrote, "We have turned to our blessings often for guidance and hope.... Each time we have used our blessings, we have received a greater insight into the things contained within them." She then listed several benefits from using our blessings:

+ Learning to use a patriarchal blessing is also a lesson in learning to receive personal revelation.
+ We draw closer to our Father in Heaven as we reach for Him and yearn to understand more clearly what He sent us to earth to do.
+ Our patriarchal blessing helps us learn how to put our lives in His hands if we will use it as the tool it was meant to be.
+ We can find answers to questions that come up.
+ We can take heed and watch for the things we are warned about.

+ We can receive the hope that can come from this study.
+ As we desire to understand, Heavenly Father teaches us how to better use the things He has given us expressly to help us make it safely through this life.
+ As with going to the temple, the more we use it, the more we understand what it is all about. (L.P.)

In innumerable ways, our patriarchal blessings benefit us.

## WARNINGS

As a specific way to guide us, patriarchal blessings often give warnings. Sometimes these are for physical dangers. A wife told of a terrifying, recurring dream—the small mobile home where she lived with her family was engulfed in flames. "I couldn't shake the feeling of foreboding," she said, and she recalled a line in her patriarchal blessing saying she would be warned and protected from harm. She insisted they move. A week later the trailer unexplainably burned to the ground.[33]

Usually warnings are of a spiritual nature. In an article designed to help parents guide their children successfully through the teen years to the temple, Joy Saunders Lundberg wrote: "When I was a teenager, I remember gaining strength from reading my patriarchal blessing. I encouraged our children to do the same. The promises and warnings given in patriarchal blessings can help youth keep an eternal perspective."[34]

A mother of seven children said her children's blessings "said things they never would have listened to me if I had told them." A warning, she said, "means I need to be strong for certain things." (E.B.) She compared warnings in our blessings to the way an earthly parent warns a child.

An Italian woman received her patriarchal blessing when she was twenty-three. She wrote:

> At that time I was a young student. I was single and very strong in the Church.... I did not have any problem in keeping any commandment. What surprised me of my patriarchal blessing was reading about the Word of Wisdom. The Lord, through the patriarch, was warning me to pay a

*special attention to the Word of Wisdom. I laughed. I said to myself, "Why the Word of Wisdom? I don't have any problem with that. I will never smoke, never drink coffee, nor alcohol." I was relying on my flesh.*

*Years went by. I got married to a nonmember. My life started changing. I was not happy with my husband. I started not attending the Church, although I never denied the testimony. I started feeling alone. I started drinking coffee. I even tried some cigarettes.*

*Suddenly I realized that Satan was attacking me on those weaknesses that I did not even know I had. The words in my patriarchal blessing came to my mind, and I repented. Now my testimony of the patriarchal blessing is stronger because of this sad experience. (T.M.)*

Rather than be embarrassed or offended by warnings in our blessings, we should be grateful to our Heavenly Father that He loves us enough to try to help us see potential problems. In a sense, these warnings are like detour signs around the potholes of life. He sees weaknesses we may not even be aware of. We do not have to take the bumpy roads in life; we can follow directions around them.

Many of our warnings are to guard our youthful years; others we should watch for throughout our lives. "These are important enough for the patriarch to mention," said one patriarch. "Most come with a promise. Warnings come in many different ways, many times in a positive way such as to be a peacemaker." (H.I.)

The Doctrine and Covenants teaches us about warnings. Many early Saints received specific warnings from the Lord. One was Emma Smith who was cautioned, "Beware of pride." (D&C 25:14.) In modern language, if a mother wants to warn her child, she yells, "Look out!" This is the exact meaning of "Beware!" Then the Lord gave the alternatives: "Keep my commandments continually, and a crown of righteousness thou shalt receive. And except thou do this, where I am you cannot come." (D&C 25:15.) This is basically the choice the Lord gives us with the forewarnings in our blessings.

One father related that his now-grown daughter had earlier

received a "beautiful blessing," but one with a warning. Later she did what she was warned against. We, too, have the choice. One college girl said, "My patriarchal blessing warns me of those who would try to lead me astray. I'm thankful for that insight so that I know I need to be strong." (K.C.D.) We can study our blessings and make a list of the "Look out!"'s. If we will heed His warnings, we can avoid the dangers. We can use our blessings to create happiness.

# DECISIONS

We can use our blessings to help us make decisions. A college student acknowledged, "I definitely could not have made them on my own." (T.T.K.) Here is a simple example of how it works. A teenage girl decided against going to a party after a Sunday School lesson quoted a scripture that was in her patriarchal blessing.[35]

Stories of young men going on missions because of their blessings are common. A young man in France was promised that "'he would have the maturity to choose his wife after serving a mission. At the time, he had already decided to get married and not go on a mission. After much prayer, he decided to go on a mission first.'" [36]

A mother said that her daughter's patriarchal blessing states she will go on a mission before motherhood. Although a striking girl with many friends, she never has had lots of dates. She is dating a strong Catholic. She is going on a mission shortly. The mother said, "I'm glad her patriarchal blessing prepared her to go on a mission. It saved her from heartaches." (C.R.#2)

When a young sister faced decisions after returning from her mission, she said, "'I read my patriarchal blessing prayerfully, and the answers were there. I'm still not entirely sure just where my path will lead, but I am sure that I am doing what the Lord wants me to do.'"[37]

A father said that his oldest daughter doesn't enjoy college life, but her patriarchal blessing tells her to continue her education. If it were not in the blessing, she would not want to, but because it's in the blessing she does. (A.A.) This is another example of using our blessings to make a decision that we would probably not make on our own and therefore would suffer a different outcome.

The mother of the college girl shared how she learned to use her blessing to make decisions.

*It has helped me make three big decisions in my life. Without it I don't know if I would have made them with clarity. The first was my marriage.*

*I had not read my blessing for many years. It said that I would marry in the temple. The words took on a different meaning when I saw them as a criteria. I asked the man I was dating one question. I knew with certainly. The clue was in my blessing. It was the first time I had used my blessing to make a decision. A very poignant experience. From that, I've used it for many decisions in my life. (E.A.)*

Another mother said she used her blessing "as a self-checklist when making a major decision." (D.I.) It's an example to follow.

## OCCUPATION

Occasionally a patriarchal blessing will state a person's occupation, even though the recipient is a youth and has not yet chosen one. One lady reported that her blessing said she would become a nurse. She had done so. (T.T.M.)

One young woman at age twenty had two years toward a degree in elementary education, but "that direction did not seem right." She applied and was accepted into a strenuous practical nursing program. Shortly after passing state board exams with higher scores than expected, she read her blessing and "was amazed at a part that seemed to jump off the page." Although it did not say she would be a nurse, she realized she was entering the right profession. (E.I.)

One young married man in college changed his major after receiving his blessing. Although his blessing did not specifically say he would be a teacher, it did mention his teaching young people. Because of this, he decided to become a teacher. He enjoys fulfillment in his career for it matches his talents. (V.D.)

A talented young mother returned to college part-time, seeking an art degree. Although aware that art may not provide an adequate living, she is not concerned. The reason: her blessing counsels her to pursue the education she wants. She enjoys the classes and refines her abilities with faith that she is making the right choice. (L.R.)

These people are following the counsel of President Ezra Taft Benson who said:

> I am glad Beethoven found his way into music, Rembrandt into art, Michelangelo into sculpturing, and President David O. McKay into teaching. To find your proper niche and do well at it can bless you, yours, and your fellowmen. If you need help in finding your career, it is available: Ponder and pray about it; study closely your patriarchal blessing; consider what you do well.... [38]

## SPIRITUAL GIFTS AND TALENTS

One brother commented, "We need to look in our patriarchal blessings and seek after the spiritual gifts that are there." (S.D.) The Lord makes it clear that "every man is given a gift by the Spirit of God." (D&S 46: 11.) Studying Doctrine and Covenants section 46 gives us insight if we have trouble with this concept.[39] Are we trying to find, develop, and use our gifts? Doing so is essential to accomplish our missions in life.

One sister said, "My patriarchal blessing advised me to listen to the Spirit.... I rejoice as I learn to freely respond to His influence." (R.I.#2)

We often define the gift of discernment as the ability to see the difference between right and wrong. But look at this example describing President Thomas S. Monson:

> Once, he 'knew' a certain bishop with whom he had shaken hands was to be a patriarch. Repeatedly he has had similar experiences, reflecting a promise in his patriarchal blessing that he would have "the spirit of discernment." But such revelatory insights are not limited to the call of leaders. It is not uncommon for him to receive this inspiration as he counsels, talks on the telephone, or considers personal action to be taken. It is a spiritual gift he has received in abundance.[40]

One woman's blessing told her she would have the spirit of discernment, but "I couldn't see it in my life," she said. "Meanwhile, I discovered that I often 'sensed' or 'knew' things especially when listening to people talk about their problems. I seemed to have insight into things that other people weren't seeing. I finally realized this was a type of discernment, and it was a blessing because through it I could bless lives. I guess that's why I had the gift." (J.T.#2)

One day a young mother decided to read in the scriptures about gifts of the Spirit before reading her blessing. The Spirit told her she needed paper and pencil. Then when she read her blessing, she "learned many things" about her gifts. "Now I see my gifts," she said. "I tell myself, yes, I have this one. I'm growing in that one. I'll have this one one day. I used to feel I didn't have any." (R.I.#2)

Similarly, a young woman thought she didn't have any talents, "but my patriarchal blessing listed them," she said. (N.D.) Finding them, like discovering spiritual gifts, is more likely a process. A missionary said, "As I studied the scriptures and my patriarchal blessing, prayed fervently, and had various missionary experiences, several of my talents were made known to me."[41]

Elder David B. Haight said, "Never underestimate what you can become or how your talents may eventually be used."[42] Recognizing our talents and spiritual gifts helps us determine our purpose in life.

## LEARNING WHO YOU ARE

A woman of many talents shared this experience:

*Many years ago I was called as Young Women counselor in the stake. President Harold B. Lee came to the stake conference. He was President of the Twelve at the time. I was waiting to be set apart, sitting on the couch. President Lee came over and said, "Who are you?"*

*I said, "Sister _____."*

*He said, "I know. I've known you before."*

*I said, "I guess I've met you at General Conference."*

*He said, "No, Sister _____."*

*He set other people apart. Then he said, "I can't set you apart, but I can assist." Afterward he came around in front of me and said, "It's so good to see you again."*

*My brother said, "He knew you on the other side."*

*Me? To rub elbows with an Apostle?*

*My brother said, "Quit putting yourself down." (N.S.)*

Like her, most of us "put ourselves down." We don't know who we are. We can't remember.

Satan knows you can't remember, and he doesn't want you to find out. "Because you are being bombarded with so many incorrect messages about who you are," your patriarchal blessing is crucial.[43] Ponder it. Seek to know who you are in your Father's eyes. He knows you. The promise is, "Ask, and it shall be given you; seek, and ye shall find; knock and it shall be opened unto you." (Luke 11:9.) Your blessing is a window to see into eternity.

A teenage boy said, "I got my patriarchal blessing in my junior year. I learn new things from it all the time. After receiving my blessing, I looked up and patriarch [Smith] was crying. I realized it wasn't him talking to me. It was Heavenly Father. ... From then on I tried to be good. ... I love the Lord very much. It helped me catch a vision of who I am and what I can be." (K.C.#2)

As Elder Neal A. Maxwell said, "'How can we truly understand who we are unless we know who we were and what we have the power to become?'"[44]

Consider this question: "If the Lord sees greatness in you, how then should you see yourself?"[45] Doesn't He know you better than you know yourself? What if, when you looked in a mirror, you could see what Heavenly Father sees? Our patriarchal blessings act as this mirror, reflecting the qualities Heavenly Father sees in us. We can study that image to learn our divine nature.

Looking in this mirror, a new mother said, "reminds me who I am. It's a great boost when I need it." (K.I.) An experienced mother observed, "My blessing has sustained me throughout many trials because my Heavenly Father has told me how He felt about me." (C.N.)

A young returned sister missionary said, "President Ezra Taft Benson in his talk on pride asked 'What will God think of me?' My patriarchal blessing says what God does think of me." (N.D.)

When we see what God thinks of us, we catch a vision of who we are, and we change how we see ourselves.

# SELF-WORTH

Our feelings of self-worth are closely aligned with our view of who we are. Our ability to love and value ourselves grows as our vision widens. A Relief Society teacher asked, "How can we use our patriarchal blessings to help us become more self-accepting?" Speaking from experience, a sister answered, "I use mine to give me a boost. I see what I can become." (N.C.)

A Young Woman said, "When I'm feeling down I go to a quiet place and read my blessing.... Each time I read it I see something new." (M.E.) In a similar way, a woman commented, "When I feel down, I turn to my patriarchal blessing which tells me that Heavenly Father loves me. I know He loves everyone, but this tells me that He loves me. It makes me feel special." (M.V.T.)

Yet another woman shared that through her blessing she is "reminded I'm of worth and that He knows I'm here." (N.K.#1) A mother of a beautiful, talented daughter said, "Even with all these things going for her she often fights low self-esteem. I prayed that taking her to get her patriarchal blessing when she was fourteen would help. I couldn't have been more right." (K.E.)

A young woman who had been a child abuse victim described how she had "'felt a gnawing emptiness, a pain that would not heal.'"

"When this young woman was in college, she found a source of healing in the form of her patriarchal blessing: 'Suddenly I knew God loved me, despite my past, and that there was a purpose for me. I began to feel a confidence in myself and in the future.'"[46] Thus, one major way that we can use our blessings is to increase our sense of self-worth.

Devastated by the death of his father who was his best friend, an eleven year old boy developed ulcers. Suffering private daily agony throughout his teenage years, he knew he "couldn't make it" without his father because he was "too dumb and too ugly." For six excruciating years, the crushing pain shredded his self-esteem.

"At seventeen," he said, "I went to the patriarch. He was an old man 80 years old; I didn't know him. When I went, I stood outside his house, and I froze. I really thought when he put his hands on my head he would say 'I'm sorry, I don't have a blessing for you.'" After fifteen anguished minutes, he "finally decided to face it."

Then, he said, "I had a marvelous experience. I felt he gave me the wrong blessing.... He told me things I knew would never happen." The patriarch also spoke to thoughts in his heart that only Heavenly Father could know. "It was as though Heavenly Father had said '... live up to your potential.'"

The boy, who once stayed home because he couldn't face giving a talk in church, today is a dynamic priesthood leader. "Impossible" promises have become reality. Receiving his patriarchal blessing transformed his life because he realized his great worth. (T.R.)

Feeling he lived less than he could, a teenager prayed mightily the week before receiving his blessing. He went with trepidation. The blessing came with power. He compared it to the experience of Enos. He saw how deeply his Father treasured him. Our Father sees our potential and our worth. He loves us. He loves you.

## OUR FATHER'S LOVE

"God loves and cares about all of his children, even when we aren't living up to our potential," wrote a sister who had not been active.[47] One night her house caught fire. "'You were lucky,'" the fireman exclaimed as he told her how quickly it could have burned down; but, he added, "'You were warned of the danger in time to avoid it.'"

She continued, "That last sentence gave me pause. Where had I heard those words before? Then I remembered; a line in my patriarchal blessing reads, "You will be warned of danger in time to avoid it." Stunned by such a direct fulfillment of a patriarchal promise, I knew then as never before that God loves me unconditionally. It was humbling to know that he was mindful of my needs even when I'd distanced myself from him."[48]

The overwhelming feelings of God's love led her back into Church activity.

A young man leaving on his mission shared his experience.

*When I received my patriarchal blessing I felt a flood of love and power overcome my whole body.... The overwhelming feeling deep within my bosom which radiated throughout my being was a pure, powerful love. This love was unmistakably from my Heavenly Father. In feeling His all encompassing love, I knew He cares for me.... My Heavenly Father loved me, and knew who I was.... I want to feel my Father's all encompassing love forever. (F.L.G.)*

Many of us have similar tear-filled memories. We can also feel our Father's love flow through us whenever we read our blessings if we will read seeking His Spirit. "'I love to read my patriarch blessing,' says Susan. 'It is like a letter from home. When I read it, I always feel loved and accepted.'"[49]

Regardless of what we don't understand or use in our blessings, we can bask in our Father's love. If this were the only blessing we received through the patriarchal paper, it would be priceless indeed. Feeling His love is reason enough to return to our blessings again and again. His love will bless our lives. As we feel our Father's love, we want to love Him too. This love motivates us to live our lives as He does—with love. Then, perhaps unknowingly, we have used our blessings in the very best of ways.

## WITHIN THE FAMILY

One universal purpose of earth life is to build righteous families. Because of that, we can use patriarchal blessings not only for ourselves but within our families. Viewed as a letter from a heavenly parent, earthly parents can use it to help them in parenting. As one mother said, "I have been amazed as I have listened to my children's blessings with how personal and individual each blessing is. God knows my children even better than I do."[50]

A woman with grown children said, "I have used not only my own but my husband's and children's patriarchal blessings to keep my mind focused on positive traits and possibilities. Whenever I get discouraged with them or find myself fault-finding, I pull out their blessings and remind myself of how the Lord sees them."

On one occasion, she "sat down with a grown son and encouraged him to study of copy of his blessing, marking in different colors: (1) warnings, (2) strengths, (3) promised blessings. He was amazed how many specifics he had never noticed before and mentioned in a later testimony on fast Sunday how much that had helped him." (E.J.)

One father has a copy of all of his family's blessings in his planner and reads them occasionally. He counsels individually with the children monthly and brings up their blessings in these counsels. One child was concerned about his blessing after getting it. It bothered him—too much to do. He couldn't do it. Later on the father did a "status check" to see how the son was feeling and if he was discouraged.

He also reads their patriarchal blessing with them if they are having problems and encourages them to read it on their own. When the missionary son wrote he was discouraged because he was trying so hard without success, the father wrote back and reminded him of phrases from his blessing.

The father said, "I don't look at life just as a test. It's an opportunity to grow. If we take time to review our blessings, we can be better prepared. We study and ponder the scriptures. We should do the same with our blessings. We can ask: 'What is there that I can use more than just reading it?'" (A.A.) It's a question to ponder.

Using patriarchal blessings can also sweeten the primary relationship of husband and wife, but we cannot always predict the process. One woman wrote:

> I had been feeling disgusted with the slow progress my husband was making spiritually while feeling smugly superior in my own diligence. After reading his blessing, I was overcome with its beauty and promises. The number of gifts mentioned and the Lord's obvious confidence in this man to use the difficult experiences of his life in positive ways brought tears to my eyes.
>
> At the dinner table I read him some of the things I had underlined in his blessing and expressed my love for him. The tone in our home changed markedly, and I was humbled to remember how different the Lord's perspective is from ours. I

*feel a need to repent of my self-righteousness and I'm determined*
*to review our blessings often. (E.G.)*

She learned, like the father in the previous story, that we can use patriarchal blessings to propel follow-up action, even if this sometimes takes an unexpected twist.

## RECOGNIZING FULFILLMENT

Being thoroughly familiar with our patriarchal blessings is the first step to recognizing the fulfillment of a specific blessing within them. Telling of a conversation with an Institute teacher, one student wrote, "I thought how his parting comment fit into my patriarchal blessing—and how if I hadn't been reading it, I never would have recognized that." (J.T.#2)

A man said, "I have seen it fulfilled. So my faith has strengthened indeed where the veil has dropped and the Spirit has been close, so powerful in directly fulfilling a line [in my blessing]. Some things are fatherly counsel to a son—good counsel. He has guided me. Things can change dramatically in a hurry." (R.I.#1)

Fulfillment can be simple, sometimes small and almost overlooked. A counselor in a bishopric said his patriarchal blessing gave him protection, which he had seen "many times." Recently he was driving by the fairgrounds when—thud—he thought he'd been hit by a bird he didn't see. But instead, it was "an egg somebody threw at me," he said. "The velocity chipped the paint on the car. It almost hit me. If it had come through the open window and hit me in the eye, the outcome would have been much different. I instantly thought of my patriarchal blessing. I didn't see divine intervention, but I am grateful for the hand of the Lord." (K.A.)

Other times we see profound fulfillment. "I have hair raising stories," said one woman, "of the many times I have been protected from evil." These were sacred, direct fulfillment of repeated promises in her blessing. (L.N.)

Another couple saw protection from danger.

*When my husband and I were first in the Church thirteen*
*years ago, his patriarchal blessing stunned both of us. We were*
*in our early thirties and though I had traveled all over the*

*world, my husband had never been out of the United States. His blessing contained the unusual statement, "You will be protected wherever you go in the world." Then the patriarch stopped and looked at us and emphasized again, "Wherever!"*

*We laughed because at the age of thirty-three with two small children, it was unlikely we would be vacationing anywhere exotic any time soon! Within a year, he went to India and Singapore for a job. Within five years, he had become the director of the international projects unit at the [university].*

*My husband travels to very dangerous third world countries two or three times a year, sometimes six or seven. He goes to places where travelers are warned not to travel— Turkey, Hungary, Micronesia. I never worry about him when he is on one of these dangerous trips. Our last name puts him in extra danger when he travels to Arab countries. His blessing was a comfort to both of us, but especially to me who is left at home to raise the children.*

*Now when he goes to the Circle K, I sometimes worry— but never when he is overseas! (K.H.)*

A sister whose blessing promised husband and family was still unmarried in her thirties. She realized these promises might not happen during mortality. "Although I understood that if worthy and faithful, I would eventually enjoy every blessing, I was still troubled," she said. "I wondered whether I could be happy if marriage and family did not come in the ways I had desired. During one difficult period, I went often to the temple. On one occasion, I was given a clear message from God. I was told that I did not need to be afraid.... As it turned out, I did marry."[51]

Another sister whose blessing promised a husband was also still unmarried in her thirties. Visits to her bishop over a period of years told her to be patient. Eventually a personal answer came that her blessing would be fulfilled after this life. At peace, she lives a rich life relying on and preparing for her future. (K.M.G.)

Patriarchs see their personal blessings come to fruition too. One said that words in his blessing were the exact words used by the

Apostle who set him apart as a patriarch. (H.A.K.)

Sometimes fulfillment comes through another. The patriarchal blessing of Juan Santos of Uruguay said that "'I would serve a mission in the temple before leaving this life. At that time there were still no temples in South America, and I had always felt that it was impossible for this promise to be fulfilled." In time, however, "a beloved returned missionary ... offered to supplement our savings so that we could go." [52]

Sometimes fulfillment of a blessing comes rather quickly, as this sister experienced.

*I was coming home from General Conference in 1969 and drove ten hours straight. I was spiritually up. All the way home there was a thought in my mind, "Get your patriarchal blessing." I did.*

*I had been schizophrenic and seriously ill for twelve years and had a terrible experience in the mental hospital in 1957 with 90 electric shock treatments. Six months after the blessing I had to go to the hospital again and was afraid the experience would be the same. One line in the blessing ... and faith in my bishop (I had been a member eighteen months) gave me the courage to go to the hospital. No more shock treatments, just medication and I was out in two weeks. (T.M.O.)*

Sometimes miracles seem to occur to bring a promise to reality. By age eighty, Hungarian Johann Denndörfer had been denied a passport seven consecutive years. How fervently he wanted to go to the temple, but he was ill and discouraged. After a month-long hospital stay, he was visited by his home teacher, a newly ordained patriarch who gave him a patriarchal blessing. It promised he would go to the temple before he died. Afterward the patriarch "worried about such a promise to an old man," but within months the passport was approved. He received his endowment in the Swiss Temple—plus doing temple work for 785 ancestors. [53]

Other times a blessing unfolds slowly over time.

*While serving in the England Bristol mission as president, one of our English missionaries came into our mission with a terrible stuttering handicap who came because he had faith in the patriarchal blessing. The patriarch had promised him that if he would fulfill an honorable mission his handicap would be overcome and he would come home as normal as anyone.*

*He was a wonderful elder keeping all mission rules and worked harder than most missionaries. For about six months he struggled through but determined to follow his blessing and do his part by exercising his faith. Because of his wonderful attitude I decided to let him be a senior and help another elder who seemed to have a psychological problem. At the same time I had the Church's psychologist visit with him and told him of the other elder's stuttering problem. The psychologist suggested he help both elders. After working with one elder, he gave the stuttering elder four or five suggestions.*

*The suggestions had to be up to the elder to be diligent in following these corrections. Such things were to slow down his speech and to substitute easier words for those that seem to bother him. Gradually we could see a difference and six months later I had him training new elders which he loved to do and he taught them how to work and keep the mission rules.*

*In eighteen months his speech was nearly normal and when he was released he bore a beautiful testimony. He was a great missionary and by following the blessing by the patriarch he was healed of his handicap and he has become a successful man in business and a father in Zion. (S.B.R.)*

Hope for actually receiving our promises comes from faith in them. A woman wrote, "I believe every word of my blessing and have lived to see many of the promises come true. I am sincerely trying to live so that the remainder of the promises will materialize." (I.H.D.) A high councilman said, "Things in my blessing have come to pass or will come to pass." (K.T.#2) This type of hope—no, faith— gives us incentive to "hang in there." A sixteen-year-old expressed the idea this way: "If we remain righteous, the blessings promised to us can be like a candle of hope lighting the way through the storms of life."[54]

Sometimes those storms require a sacrifice to obtain the promised blessing. A wife wrote:

*My mother-in law's blessing told her she'd have sons and daughters. After she married she had a quick succession of one boy and five girls. When her last girl was just a baby, she was in a severe car accident that left her knee and hip broken. She had several surgeries and was bedridden for quite some time. Of course her doctors told her that more children were out of the question. She couldn't possibly carry a baby with a broken hip—plus it would make her hip worse.*

*My mother-in-law believed her patriarchal blessing, however, and knew she was supposed to have another son. She did get pregnant again and knew while she was carrying him he'd be a boy.*

*Years later, after my husband's family had moved across the country, my husband got his patriarchal blessing. The patriarch, whom I assume didn't know about my husband's past, told him he had covenanted with his parents in the premortal existence to come down to them.*

*I look at my wonderful husband and my two beautiful children and I'm very thankful my mother-in-law had the faith in her blessing and was willing to make the sacrifices she did to bring my husband to her family. She still uses crutches to get around more than 35 years later. (K.S.)*

If we think of life as an open book test, our patriarchal blessings become the personalized text to read, underline, and refer to. But rather than an answer book, with rote, prescribed answers, a patriarchal blessing is more like a lab workbook with conditions to work through and solutions to discover. By following the proper process we come to know the answers.

The more we use our blessings, the more we will know how to use them to bless our lives. President Gordon B. Hinckley said, "You cannot make it alone. You cannot reach your potential alone. You need the help of the Lord."[55]

We have patriarchal blessings so we can have—and use—the help of the Lord.

# SOURCES

1. Eldred G. Smith, *Conference Report*, Apr. 1960, p. 66.

2. *Webster's Ninth New Collegiate Dictionary*, Springfield: Merriam-Webster Inc., 1984, p. 660, definition 2.

3. Joseph Fielding Smith, comp., *Teachings of the Prophet Joseph Smith*, Salt Lake City: Deseret Book Co., 1977, p. 159.

4. Bruce R. McConkie, *The Promised Messiah*, Salt Lake City: Deseret Book Co., 1978, p. 27.

5. Sheri L. Dew, "This Is a Test. It Is Only a Test," *Ensign*, July 2000, p. 65.

6. Eldred G. Smith, *Conference Report*, Apr. 1960, p. 66.

7. John A. Widtsoe, *Evidences and Reconciliations*, Salt Lake City: Bookcraft, 1943, p. 76.

8. Edward L. Kimball, ed., *Teachings of Spencer W. Kimball*, Salt Lake City: Bookcraft, 1982, p. 505.

9. Harold B. Lee, *Stand Ye In Holy Places*, Salt Lake City: Deseret Book Co., 1988, p. 117; quoting Karl G. Maeser.

10. Eldred G. Smith, *Conference Report*, Apr. 1960, p. 66.

11. Thomas S. Monson, "Preparation Precedes Performance," *Ensign*, Sept. 1993, p. 71.

12. Lynn A. Mickelsen, "Light and Growth," *Ensign*, Sept. 2004, p. 9.

13. Edward L. Kimball, ed., *Teachings of Spencer W. Kimball*, Salt Lake City: Bookcraft, 1982, p. 505.

14. Ezra Taft Benson, *Teachings of Ezra Taft Benson*, Salt Lake City: Bookcraft, 1988, p. 214.

15. Eldred G. Smith, *Conference Report*, Apr. 1953, p. 30.

16. John A. Widtsoe, *Evidences and Reconciliations*, Salt Lake City: Bookcraft, 1943, p. 74.

17. "To The Young Women of the Church," *Ensign*, Nov. 1986, p. 82.

18. Ezra Taft Benson, *Teachings of Ezra Taft Benson*, Salt Lake City: Bookcraft, 1988, p. 214.

19. "Gaining Strength through Patriarchal Blessings," *Ensign*, June 1994, p. 53.

20. "Q&A" *New Era*, Mar. 1992, p. 18.

21. Julie B. Beck, "You Have a Noble Birthright," *Ensign*, May 2006, p. 107.

22. "Remember Also the Promises," *Ensign*, Nov. 1992, p. 80.

23. Gerald E. Melchin, "'Thy Sins Are Forgiven,'" *Ensign*, Jan. 1995, p. 20.

24. Kellene Ricks Adams, "Alone for the Holidays," *Ensign*, Dec. 1996, p. 21.

25. "Q&A" *New Era*, Mar. 1992, p. 19.

26. "Q&A" *New Era*, Mar. 1992, p. 18.

27. Marleen S. Williams, "Raising a Child with a Disability," *Ensign*, Oct. 2004, p. 16.

28. Julie B. Beck, "You Have a Noble Birthright," *Ensign*, May 2006, p. 106.

29. Michael R. Morris, "Welcome Home!" *Ensign*, Dec. 1994, p. 37.

30. "'Faithful, Good, Virtuous, True' Pioneers in the Philippines," *Ensign*, Aug. 1997, pp. 59-60.

31. Celia Augusto de Souza, "'Read Your Patriarchal Blessing!'" *Ensign*, Dec. 2003, p. 62.

32. "The Journey to Healing," *Ensign*, Sept. 1997, p. 22.

33. Patricia Tarrant, "Forewarned by a Dream," *Ensign*, Mar. 1993, pp. 64-65.

34. "It's a Date," *Ensign*, June 1992, p. 26.

35. Don L. Searle, "Tudo Bem in Brazil," *Ensign*, Mar. 1997, p. 44.

36. LaRene Porter Gaunt, "A Blooming in France," *Ensign*, Mar. 1995, p. 49.

37. "Gaining Strength through Patriarchal Blessings," *Ensign*, June 1994, p. 53.

38. "In His Steps," 1979 Devotional Speeches of the Year, Provo, Utah: BYU, 1980, pp. 64-65; also Ezra Taft Benson, *Teachings of Ezra Taft Benson*, Salt Lake City: Bookcraft, 1988, pp. 484-485.

39. See Robert D. Hales, "Gifts of the Spirit," *Ensign*, Feb. 2002, pp. 12-20.

40. Francis M. Gibbons, "President Thomas S. Monson," *Ensign*, July 1995, p. 11.

41. Ronald A. Rasband, "The Talents," *Ensign*, Aug. 2003, p. 34.

42. David B. Haight, "A Time for Preparation," *Ensign*, Nov. 1991, p. 38.

43. Julie B. Beck, "You Have a Noble Birthright," *Ensign*, May 2006, p. 106.

44. Hal G. Ferguson, "I Have a Question," *Ensign*, Jan. 1995, p. 61; quoting *Ensign*, May 1986, p. 35.

45. L. Tom Perry, "Youth of the Noble Birthright," *Ensign*, Nov. 1998, p. 74.

46. Maxine Murdock, "Hope and Healing," *Ensign*, Jan. 1993, p. 67.

47. Jackie Ireland, "Is There Any Reason You Can't Come to Church?" *Ensign*, July 1992, p. 22.

48. Ibid.

49. "Gaining Strength through Patriarchal Blessings," *Ensign*, June 1994, p. 53.

50. "Gaining Strength through Patriarchal Blessings," *Ensign*, June 1994, p. 53.

51. Inouye, Jeanne, "'Be of Good Cheer,'" *Ensign*, Nov. 1993, p. 96.

52. Nestor Curbelo, "Putting Down Roots in Uruguay," *Ensign*, Dec. 1997, p. 21.

53. Douglas F. Tobler, "Alone with God," *Ensign*, Apr. 1993, p. 52.

54. "Q&A" *New Era*, Mar. 1992, p. 19.

55. Gordon B. Hinckley, "Inspirational Thoughts," *Ensign*, Aug. 1997, p. 5.

# CHAPTER 9

## Your Purpose and Mission in Life

"I challenge every one of you," said President Gordon B. Hinckley, "to rise to the divinity within you. Do we really realize what it means to be a child of God?"[1]

This challenge involves both what we will be and what we will do. We have looked through the window of our patriarchal blessings to see who we are. Now open the window to see where you fit in our Father's plan. Each of us lived and developed gifts, talents, and strengths long before we came to this earth. Our uniqueness equips us for a part in our Father's plan that only we can do, at least in the way we alone would do it. This becomes what many call our purpose or mission in life.

Some patriarchal blessings instruct the recipient that he has a particular, clearly defined assignment as his mission in life. Others seemingly say nothing about the topic. Perhaps these simply use words that the reader either misses or has difficulty interpreting. A blessing probably will not say, "Your mission in life is _____." Rather, it may speak of gifts, duties, callings, talents, responsibilities, or opportunities. These may be or may point to your mission. Generally speaking, a patriarchal blessing gives insight to your purpose in life. If we understand and use this knowledge, it will be a great help to us.

## MANKIND

The idea and concept of having a mission or calling to perform in life is not unique to members of the Church. Even the terms are used by others around us. Many years ago a man who felt life was not worth living determined to drink some poison. He went to a local park and did so. Later he looked up at the stars in amazement, wondering if he were dead. The fact that he was still alive transposed his inner life. Norman Vincent Peale, who told the man's story, wrote, "He always believed, simply, that God wanted him to do a job in life.... He made it his whole mission in life to encourage others."[2]

A news item by the Associated Press reported the comments of a former TV star. He had found "solace in God since his acquittal on charges of shooting a drug dealer. And [he], who was once a heavy cocaine user, said he hasn't touched the drug in three years. 'I've realized that all the things I do have to be done to glorify God.... It made me realize that I do have a calling and a lot of things to do.'"[3]

Apparently each person within the billions on earth has a calling or a mission to perform. Our efforts may be needed to move forward a common cause for the betterment of mankind. Even if we think we are only a small cog in a massive machine, we are critically important. The largest machine cannot work without the tiniest cog. A "small cog" can influence one life at a time, one day at a time, just as the Savior did. One screw fell out of a woman's car causing a flap to rub and put wear on her tire and creating an alarming racket. Even if we think we are a small cog or an insignificant screw, God needs us. After all, cogs make things move and screws hold things together. "Out of small things proceedeth that which is great." (D&C 64:33.) Act today to discover and fulfill your mission.

# CHURCH MEMBERS

As Church members we have a generic mission to help prepare the earth for the Second Coming of Christ. President Gordon B. Hinckley said, "When all is said and done, I remind you that this is our great mission—to bear witness to the world, both with example and precept, of the living reality of the Son of God, the resurrected Lord, who is our Redeemer and our Savior."[4]

Of this mission John A. Widtsoe, a deceased Apostle, said:

*In our preexistent state, in the day of the great council, we made a certain agreement with the Almighty. The Lord proposed a plan, conceived by him. We accepted it. Since the plan is intended for all men, we became parties to the salvation of every person under that plan. We agreed, right then and there, to be not only saviors for ourselves but measurably, saviors for the whole human family.* We went into a partnership with the Lord. *The working out of the plan became then not merely the Father's work, and the Savior's work, but also our work. The least of us, the humblest, is in partnership with the Almighty in achieving the purpose of the eternal plan of salvation.*[5]

Thus, in the premortal world we "made promises about our lives in the second estate or mortality."[6] In fact, "We are not on earth at this time by accident. [Our Father in Heaven] knows how each of us can use [our] strengths and characteristics for the building of the kingdom of God in these latter days."[7] This is the "larger purpose" of our mortal lives.

In a symbolic effort to unite in this larger purpose, the Relief Society celebrated its sesquicentennial year by rendering service in local communities. One community worker, suddenly catching the vision of Relief Societies around the world contributing such service, exclaimed, "Then you'll change the world." Elaine L. Jack, Relief Society General President at the time, reported this comment and added, "We will change the world. For the better."[8]

We, as members of the Church, unitedly and individually can change the world. This is an all-encompassing mission to us as members. This is our way to assist Christ in His mission to "bring to pass the immortality and eternal life of man." (Moses 1:39.)

# PERSONALLY AND SPECIFICALLY

Within the framework of our united, overall mission is another—smaller and more specific. A prophet clearly stated, "Each has a duty; each has a mission to perform."[9]

President Thomas S. Monson itemized the guidelines used in planning the women's Church curriculum, adding, "these have been followed with resolute care." The number one guideline read: "Every woman has been endowed by God with distinctive characteristics, gifts, and talents in order that she may fulfill a specific mission in the eternal plan."[10]

The concept is true for each of us. "Our Heavenly Father endowed His sons and daughters with unique traits especially fitted for their individual responsibilities as they fulfill His plan," said Elder Richard G. Scott. "To follow His plan requires that you do those things He expects of you as a son or daughter, husband or wife."[11]

As individuals we must come to recognize two things. First, we must believe that we actually have a personal and specific mission to accomplish. Second, we must realize that our talents directly tie into our missions.

The simplified process for finding our personal missions is explained by V. Dallas Merrell. "As people come to Christ, they develop their full potential," he observed when interviewed as a newly-sustained member of the Second Quorum of Seventy. "Each of us grows as we find out the talents and gifts that we have and then learns to submit to the Father's will about how to use those during our sojourn on earth."[12]

At a BYU devotional some years ago, Elder John H. Groberg went into detail:

> What is your mission in life? What does God expect you to accomplish ...? And are you doing it?
>
> I hope ... we can all realize ... the importance of at least three things: first, that God, our Father in Heaven, does have a specific mission for all of us to fulfill and perform ... second, that we can, here and now in this life, discover what that mission is; and third, that with His help we can fulfill that mission....
>
> If we do not know what our mission is, if we are not sure, if we are uncertain as to whether we are in fact fulfilling it ... then it does not really matter what else we are spending our time doing.... Or to put it another way, if we are really interested in doing our Father's will we had better pay the price—whatever price is necessary.[13]

Elder Groberg went on to address this question: How do we know what our life's mission is?

> Such a revelation will not come all at once. God will unfold it to us line upon line, according to what is best for us and how capable we are of handling it, and what is best for the progress of his work. But remember that you must start somewhere....
>
> While every person must ultimately receive his own revelation and assurance ..., there are great helps available to us ... in discovering what our mission in this life is. I use the word "discover" advisedly, for it connotes the correct feeling of something that already exists but needs to be found.[14]

According to Elder Groberg, the most important thing we must do to discover our calling in life is to "follow the Savior." He then reviewed some specific ways to do this. "Obtain your patriarchal blessing," he advised; "or, if you already have it, study it carefully and prayerfully yourself—not necessarily with others."[15]

A man who grew up as a nonmember without religious influence nonetheless had a special relationship with his Heavenly Father. Finding his purpose was a process. He related:

> In my youth, I had survived car wrecks, fires, [parents'] divorce, being stung by a Japanese man-of-war, gangs, and more. By the time I was thirteen years old, I was convinced that I could not die because God had other plans for me.
>
> By the time I started regular dating, I was searching for the one true church so that I could pay back my Heavenly Father. I wasn't totally aware of what it was He needed me to do, but I did know I was here for a purpose....
>
> The instant that I first heard about receiving a patriarchal blessing, a voice went off in my head. This voice said, "This is how Heavenly Father can talk to you personally. If you want to know what to do with your life, this is what you need." ...
>
> I knew all along that my Heavenly Father loved me, but I was confused at many of the life and death situations that I had been put in. Now I knew I wasn't just here for me. I was sent here to be the father of my children. My experiences were

*for their benefit as well. This one thought has changed the way I dated, the way I worked, the way I look at all trials that come upon me....*

*I know with no doubt in my mind that my Father loves me and that my life has purpose. (V.B.H.)*

Former General Relief Society President Elaine L. Jack shared her method for finding her mission. She also discovered rewards in the process.

*We discover what our own life tasks are by asking the right questions. Perhaps the most important question we can ask is, 'What is the Lord's will for me?' That is our gauge for progression ... The answers I have found as I've asked about my own mission and path of progression have brought boundless stability to my life. They have given me a sense of purpose and vision, a sustaining nourishment of body and soul."*[16]

Sister Jack testified of her belief in a mission for each one of us. "We know His promises are real, that He does know us by name and has a plan for each of us. He will help us learn what it is and give us joy in doing it."[17] He will help us; he will help you because "You are loved more than you will ever know. He wants you to be successful in your life's mission!"[18]

# EXAMPLES

President Spencer W. Kimball shared that he had a special calling to preach to the Lamanites. But we do not have to be a President Kimball to have a special assignment or to figure out what it is.

If we follow the Spirit, it will lead us to where we need to be. Because a Fiji native followed the Spirit, he and his wife moved to Hawaii; there he was asked to help translate the temple ordinances into Fijian. Later, again not knowing why, he followed the Spirit by moving to Utah. This time he was asked to help voice the temple ordinances in Fijian. After returning to Fiji, he commented, "'Now I have to stay worthy so that I will be ready when [the Lord] needs me to fulfill another part of my mission,'"[19]

At times our patriarchal blessings point to multiple assignments.

One man changing his career said of his blessing, "Among other things it states that I have three missions in life: (1) to raise a family, (2) to serve in the missions of the Church, and (3) to assist those presently engaged in the work of salvation for my ancestors." (K.F.I.)

Sometimes our blessings lead us into uncharted paths. One energetic woman confided, "My blessing told me to work with the youth. I didn't like that." After several years of callings with the youth, she now loves it. Her blessing guided her into a mission she didn't know she had and didn't think she had the talent for. She wonders if, without the blessing, she would have had the incentive or the courage to try. (N.G.)

A woman who received a blessing after retirement stated that it gave her specific assignments. "I was instructed to pursue and develop my talents in writing, teaching, and the arts," she said. As a result:

> I lay awake nights, going over in my mind the histories of family members, friends, happenings, and articles I have tackled, and have become friends with a wonderful computer that continues to amaze me. It is my prayer that I may, in some measure, develop the talents I was sent to this earth with, to fulfill the blessing I received. (B.C.N.)

Another woman shared at some length her feelings about her mission in life.

> How many weeks, months, and years have I searched my soul, desiring to know my mission in life? How many hours were spent in tears, seeking greater insight? Every time I read my patriarchal blessing, I always felt that I have a mission to accomplish.... I wanted to be like my Savior and say, do, and be the person I should be. That was my greatest heart's desire.

She wrote of marrying and carrying the weight of not having children, yet at the same time experiencing growth, exhilarating success, even recognition in developing plans as an elementary school librarian. Then, many times, she worried:

> "Why are these projects so much more important for me than having a family?" The impression would come that I was being prepared for something the Lord wanted me to do.

After adopting a child, she experienced an extended period of depression. On hindsight, she realized, "The skills I developed pulling myself out of the depression are the very skills I need to fulfill my mission in life. I could not have acquired them any other way."

Through both daily and spiritual struggles, she has come to see "a little further ahead" in her life. From this perspective, she said:

> Someday when the time is right I will have prepared myself and the opportunities will be there.... There are talents I cultivated pre-existently and promises I made to others as well as to the Lord when I covenanted to complete my mission in this life.
>
> I feel the importance and urgency of my work. I know the ideas will only come as I work with my own family.... One afternoon as I lay reflecting ... the impression was so strong that I knew councils still meet in heaven to discuss ways to help and encourage us to fulfill our callings in life.

She believes we must work diligently to fulfill our individual missions in life. To illustrate, she told a story from her missionary days.

> One day our entire district met at a castle to proselyte. There was excitement that day because someone was getting married; we would have lots of people to talk to. As I was trying to formulate my approaches in German, I noticed one missionary whose arms were folded across his chest, smiling as he leaned against a wall. I went over to him and asked him what he was going to say. He said, "Why should I say anything?" He continued to explain that he had only three months left and then he could go home. He would have completed his mission; all he had to do was wait.
>
> This incident has often caused me to reflect and ask myself how I will feel when I meet my Savior and report on my mission in life? Will I say, "But I raised my children! What else did you expect me to do?" Or will I kneel at his feet thankful that I could also share my life, my talents, and my testimony with others? (R.I.#2)

Elder Glenn L. Pace expressed both why and how we need to carry out our personal missions.

> How tragic it will be if we don't each come to grips with our own personal potential and learn the role the Lord has in mind for us. How sad if we waste one more day with a lack of commitment and not meet the measure of our creation. When we genuinely lay everything on the altar, an illumination follows that helps us understand what our role is to be in building God's kingdom today.[20]

# OURS ALONE

Elder John H. Groberg stated that sometimes in near brushes with death, we "more clearly comprehend that there is a reason for our being here—in actuality, a mission for us to perform—and that we had better get with it."[21] A man in his fifties experienced that. He said, "A year ago I was on the floor of my den clutching my chest, watching my life go before my eyes, knowing I hadn't accomplished what I was supposed to. I prayed as hard as I've ever prayed for one more chance to serve Him. I would do it." (S.N.#2) Even without such an experience as an incentive, maybe we "had better get with it" and "do it."

Elder M. Russell Ballard remarked that he saw a bumper sticker reading: "God put me on earth to accomplish a certain number of things. Right now I am so far behind, I will never die!"[22]

President Thomas S. Monson urged us to take the matter seriously, declaring, "No assignment is menial in the work of the Lord, for each has eternal consequences." He emphasized:

> President John Taylor warned us. "If you do not magnify your calling, God will hold you responsible for those whom you might have saved had you done your duty. And who of us can afford to be responsible for the delay of eternal life of a human soul? If great joy is the reward of saving one soul, then how terrible must be the remorse of those whose timid efforts have allowed a child of God to go unwarned or unaided so that he has to wait till a dependable servant of God comes along."[23]

Indeed, one person can be critical to the eternal progress of another, and when we fall short, there are consequences. A speaker related:

> A few years ago, I spoke at a seminary graduation where there was a young Indian boy in the congregation. While he was on his mission, he taught and baptized a 73-year-old Indian woman. Right after she was baptized, she got her patriarchal blessing, and in her patriarchal blessing it told her that she should have been baptized thirty-seven years ago. But the reason she wasn't baptized was because the missionary who was supposed to baptize her refused his mission call. Young men, go on missions. Would you like to have that on your conscience for all eternity?[24]

Perhaps this story helps us realize why President Gordon B. Hinckley stated that God's "grand design cannot succeed without you."[25]

The father of a mentally disabled son realized that "in the eternal scheme of things, Adam has a different mission to fill."[26] In other words, he had a mission too. Regardless of our handicaps or weaknesses, or perhaps because of them, we each have a mission.

"Before we came to this earth, we may have been fashioned to do some small good in this life that no one else can do.... If God has a work for those with many talents, I believe he also has an important work for those of us who have few."[27]

In high school Sheri L. Dew thought she had few talents, but she loved basketball and was an unusually good player. She went to BYU intent on trying out for the women's basketball team. But when she got to the tryout door, "the confidence drained right out the bottom of her shoes." For three hours, she paced outside the door, hoping to muster the courage to walk through. She never did.

Many years later the coach told her they had played one player short all year because she couldn't find a tall center who could post up. Sister Dew said, "That was supposed to be my spot on the team. You mean out of 25,000 students they couldn't find one girl who could fill that spot?! The truth is, nobody can take your place."[28] The fact that she later served in the General Relief Society Presidency could not ease the pain of regret. Who knows why that position was hers alone? We must open the door to fill the spot on the team meant for us.

Our mission is ours alone. It's assigned to us, even reserved for us. An event in Nephi's life shows that assignments are literally reserved with our name on them, waiting for us to show up at the tryouts and claim them. Nephi, great prophet that he was, saw a marvelous vision, but he was forbidden to write the end of it because that job was reserved for someone else, an Apostle in Jesus' day. (See I Nephi 14:20-21, 25.) Our Father, treating us alike, has a specific job reserved for every one of us. But sometimes we walk the hall.

One of the Seventy, H. Burke Peterson said this:

*Have you ever thought: "I'm not very important so what I say or do will never really be noticed? ... Do I actually have any worthwhile talents? ... I'm not that special. If I don't help, someone else will come along and do a better job than I can do."*

*You were preserved to come to the earth in this time for a special purpose. Not just a few of you, but all of you. There are things for each of you to do that no one else can do as well as you. If you do not prepare to do them, they will not be done. Your mission is unique and distinctive for you. Please don't make another have to take your place. He or she can't do it as well as you can. If you will let Him, I testify that our Father in Heaven will walk with you through the journey of life and inspire you to know your special purpose here."*[29]

# THE CONDITION

We know, of course, that we have to be faithful to receive our promised blessings. "It is the continual, day-by-day, faithful living of a righteous life that will, in the end, be what the Lord requires of us.... If we do not see our lives in this way, we may become confused and frustrated about our personal life's work."[30]

One young man while on his mission learned, "The secret to eternal progression is daily progression." (Author unknown.)

The concept applies to obtaining the promises in our patriarchal blessings; they are part of our daily and eternal progress.

One young mother shared her insight on faithfulness.

*We must remember that these blessings are given to us through our faithfulness. This doesn't mean that we believe they will come to pass, so thus they will, but that we must do something to obtain them. When we read our blessings we must not only seek to know if this even will take place, but also what is required of us to bring it forth.*

*When I was a teenager I had a fear of marrying and having children because of events that had occurred in my life. I was afraid that I would not be a suitable mother. My patriarchal blessing said that I would have a family, that I would be a mother in Israel, and that my children would call me blessed. This calmed my fears for a time.*

*Yet, I soon came to wonder what the word faithfulness meant. It is contained in a sentence in the last paragraph of my blessing, as it is in everyone's. This word implies that all of these things may or may not come to pass, depending on me. So what does it mean?*

*Two scriptures demonstrating the meaning of this word come to mind. The first is 1 Ne. 3:16. It reads: "Let us be faithful in keeping the Lord's commandments." Can we keep the commandments merely by believing them? No, it takes action on our beliefs.*

*D&C 81:5 reads: "Wherefore, be faithful; stand in the office which I have appointed unto you; succor the weak, lift up the hands which hang down, and strengthen feeble knees." All of these commandments are action commandments, therefore, doesn't being faithful require action also?*

*If faithfulness is the action principle of faith, then the commandment to be faithful is a law of doing rather than merely believing. Any blessing given through our faithfulness requires action to have it come to pass.*

*After realizing that I had to do something to become a good mother I turned again to my blessing. The conditions of this blessing were contained in the same paragraph describing my blessings in motherhood. I was told to prepare well, thoroughly learn the gospel. This was the action I needed to take. My faithfulness in doing this would bring forth the desired results.*

*There is something rather simple that we can do to find what action is required of us to obtain certain blessings. Grab a piece of paper, a pen, and your patriarchal blessing. Start from the very beginning and list each blessing that you can receive in your life. Then, search for those conditions that are given and list them beneath the corresponding blessing. Now you have a clear picture of what is required of you to obtain each blessing.*

*Of course, our patriarchal blessings also include gifts. These are given to us without conditions. However, if we do not live our lives righteously, being faithful in all things, these gifts may be diminished in our lives, if not taken completely. Faithfulness is required to magnify these talents and gifts to use them properly. The Lord expects us to magnify these gifts. We learn this in the parable of the talents. We see, then, that action is required even for the gifts we have been given.*

*When we recognize the things that we must do to obtain these great blessings in our lives we can then more fully obtain and appreciate them. Let us be more diligent and faithful in searching and understanding our patriarchal blessings. We shall then be truly blessed. (V.B.D.)*

By applying this woman's thoughts to the following scripture, we see why President Thomas S. Monson called our patriarchal blessings a liahona: "And it came to pass that I, Nephi, beheld the pointers which were in the ball, that they did work according to the faith and diligence and heed which we did give unto them." (1 Ne. 16:28.)

## ONE MORE PROMISE

Our Heavenly Father gives us a patriarchal blessing—literally a Father's blessing. A sacred friend, it guides us personally through this life and prepares us for the next. We are His children. This is not a platitude. He knows us by name—our name now, our name before, and our name after this life—because He knows who we are, who we really are. He truly wants to give us the blessings He has promised.

After all His blessings and promises, there is one more. He promises to keep his promises. "For he will fulfil all his promises which he shall make unto you, for he has fulfilled his promises which he has made unto our fathers." (Alma 37:17.) We only need to be faithful and obedient, and we will receive all the promises He has made to us. Indeed, the blessing itself "confers power upon us, if we will use it, to win the fulfillment"[31] of our promises. This is the simple yet profound power of your patriarchal blessing.

# SOURCES

1. Gordon B. Hinckley, "Each a Better Person," *Ensign*, Nov. 2002, p. 99.

2. Norman Vincent Peale, *The Amazing Results of Positive Thinking*, Englewood Cliffs, New Jersey: Prentice-Hall, Inc., 1959, pp. 261-262.

3. Tribune Newspapers, 29 Aug. 1992.

4. "Our Great Mission," *Ensign*, May 1992, p. 89.

5. "Being True to Our Foreordained Missions in the Last Days," *Come Unto Me: Relief Society Personal Study Guide 3*, Salt Lake City: The Church of Jesus Christ of Latter-day Saints, 1991, p. 61, emphasis included; quoting from "Lesson Course," *Utah Genealogical and Historical Magazine*, Oct. 1934, p. 189.

6. *Come Unto Me: Relief Society Personal Study Guide 3*, Salt Lake City: The Church of Jesus Christ of Latter-day Saints, 1991, p. 61.

7. *Ibid.*, p. 62.

8. Elaine L. Jack, "Look Up and Press On," *Ensign*, May 1992, p. 99.

9. Gordon B. Hinckley, "Our Testimony to the World," *Ensign*, May 1997, p. 84.

10. Thomas S. Monson, "The Spirit of Relief Society," *Ensign*, May 1992, p. 101.

11. Richard G. Scott, "The Joy of Living the Great Plan of Happiness," *Ensign*, Nov. 1996, p. 73.

12. "Elder V. Dallas Merrell of the Seventy," *Ensign*, Aug. 1992, p. 79.

13. John H. Groberg, "What Is Your Mission?" *BYU Speeches*, May 1979, pp. 92-93.

14. *Ibid.*, p. 93.

15. *Ibid.*

16. Elaine L. Jack, *Eye to Eye Heart to Heart*, Salt Lake City: Deseret Book Company, 1992, p. 105.

17. Elaine L. Jack, "Charity Never Faileth," *Ensign*, May 1992, p. 90.

18. Margaret D. Nadauld, "A Comforter, a Guide, a Testifier," *Ensign*, May 2001, p. 80.

19. Shirleen Meek Saunders, "In the Lord's Time," *Ensign*, June 1992, p. 70.

20. Glenn L. Pace, *Spiritual Plateaus*, Salt Lake City, Utah: Deseret Book Co., 1991, pp. 50-51.

21. John H. Groberg, "What Is Your Mission?" *BYU Speeches*, May 1979, p. 96.

22. M. Russell Ballard, "Be an Example of the Believers," *Ensign*, Nov. 1991, p. 95.

23. Thomas S. Monson, "To Learn, To Do, To Be," *Ensign*, May 1992, p. 48.

24. Ron Zeidner, "The Quest for Exaltation," Covenant Recordings, 1980, Audio Tape Cassette 1, Side A.

25. Gordon B. Hinckley, "Daughters of God," *Ensign*, Nov. 1991, p. 97.

26. Layne Potter, "'Dad, I'm Okay,'" *Ensign*, Jan. 1997, p. 65.

27. James E. Faust, "Five Loaves and Two Fishes," *Ensign*, May 1994, pp. 5-6.

28. Doug Robinson, "Living the Unexpected Life," *Deseret News*, 10 Mar. 2002, p. A7.

29. H. Burke Peterson, "Your Life Has a Purpose," *New Era*, May 1979, pp. 4-5.

30. *Come Unto Me, Relief Society Study Guide 3*, Salt Lake City: The Church of Jesus Christ of Latter-Day Saints, 1991, p. 63.

31. John A. Widtsoe, *Evidences and Reconciliations*, Salt Lake City: Bookcraft, 1943, p. 77.

# APPENDIX I

## SONS OF JACOB IN BIRTH ORDER

Reuben
Simeon
Levi
Judah
Dan
Naphtali
Gad
Asher
Issachar
Zebulun
Joseph
Benjamin

## SONS OF JACOB IN ORDER OF BLESSINGS RECEIVED

Reuben
Simeon
Levi
Judah
Zebulun
Issachar
Dan
Gad
Asher
Naphtali
Joseph
Benjamin

# SONS OF JACOB BY WIFE

(see Gen. 29:32-35; 30:1-24; 35:18)

Leah
    Reuben
    Simeon
    Levi
    Judah
    Issachar
    Zebulun

Leah's maid Zilpah
    Gad
    Asher

Rachel
    Joseph
    Benjamin

Rachel's maid Bilhah
    Dan
    Naphtali

## OR

Leah
    Reuben
    Simeon
    Levi
    Judah
    Gad – by maid Zilpah
    Asher – by maid Zilpah
    Issachar
    Zebulun

Rachel
    Dan – by maid Bilhah
    Naphtali – by maid Bilhah
    Joseph
    Benjamin

# BLESSINGS GIVEN BY JACOB

(to his 12 sons)

REUBEN, *son of Leah*

"Reuben, thou art my firstborn, my might, and the beginning of my strength, the excellency of dignity, and the excellency of power:

Unstable as water, thou shalt not excel; because thou wentest up to thy father's bed; then defiledst thou it: he went up to my couch." (Gen. 49:3-4.)

SIMEON, *son of Leah* and LEVI, *son of Leah*

"Simeon and Levi are brethren; instruments of cruelty are in their habitations.

O my soul, come not thou into their secret; unto their assembly, mine honour, be not thou united: for in their anger they slew a man, and in their selfwill they digged down a wall.

Cursed be their anger, for it was fierce; and their wrath, for it was cruel: I will divide them in Jacob, and scatter them in Israel." (Gen. 49:5-7.)

# BLESSINGS GIVEN BY MOSES

(to the 12 tribes)

REUBEN, *son of Leah*

"Let Reuben live, and not die; and let not his men be few." (Deut. 33:6.)

SIMEON, *son of Leah* and LEVI, *son of Leah*

Simeon: blessing not given.

Levi: "Let thy Thummim and thy Urim be with thy holy one, whom thou didst prove at Massah, and with whom thou didst strive at the waters of Meribah;

Who said unto his father and to his mother, I have not seen him; neither did he acknowledge his brethren, nor knew his own children: for they have observed thy word, and kept thy covenant.

They shall teach Jacob thy judgments, and Israel thy law:

## BLESSINGS BY JACOB

## BLESSINGS BY MOSES

they shall put incense before thee, and whole burnt sacrifice upon thine altar.

Bless, LORD, his substance, and accept the work of his hands: smite through the loins of them that rise against him, and of them that hate him, that they rise not again." (Duet. 33:8-11.)

JUDAH, *son of Leah*

"Judah, thou art he whom thy brethren shall praise: thy hand shall be in the neck of thine enemies; thy father's children shall bow down before thee.

Judah is a lion's whelp: from the prey, my son, thou art gone up: he stooped down, he couched as a lion, and as an old lion; who shall rouse him up?

The sceptre shall not depart from Judah, nor a lawgiver from between his feet, until Shiloh come; and unto him shall the gathering of the people be.

Binding his foal unto the vine, and his ass's colt unto the choice vine; he washed his garments in wine, and his clothes in the blood of grapes;

His eyes shall be red with wine, and his teeth white with milk." (Gen. 49:8-12.)

JUDAH, *son of Leah*

"Hear, LORD, the voice of Judah, and bring him unto his people: let his hands be sufficient for him; and be thou an help to him from his enemies." (Deut. 33:7.)

## BLESSINGS BY JACOB

ZEBULUN, *son of Leah*

"Zebulun shall dwell at the haven of the sea; and he shall be for an haven of ships; and his border shall be unto Zidon." (Gen. 49:13.)

ISSACHAR, *son of Leah*

"Issachar is a strong ass couching down between two burdens:

And he saw that rest was good, and the land that it was pleasant; and bowed his shoulder to bear, and became a servant unto tribute." (Gen. 49:14-15).

DAN, *son of Rachel's maid Bilhah*

"Dan shall judge his people, as one of the tribes of Israel.

Dan shall be a serpent by the way, an adder in the path, that biteth the horse heels, so that his rider shall fall backward.

I have waited for thy salvation, O Lord." (Gen. 49:16-18.)

GAD, *son of Leah's maid Zilpah*

"Gad, a troop shall overcome him: but he shall overcome at the last." (Gen. 49:19.)

## BLESSINGS BY MOSES

ZEBULUN, *son of Leah* and ISSACHAR, *son of Leah*

"Rejoice, Zebulun, in thy going out; and Issachar, in thy tents.

They shall call the people unto the mountain; there they shall offer sacrifices of righteousness: for they shall suck of the abundance of the seas, and of treasures hid in the sand." (Deut. 33:18-19.)

DAN, *son of Rachel's maid Bilhah*

"Dan is a lion's whelp: he shall leap from Bashan." (Deut. 33:22.)

GAD, *son of Leah's maid Zilpah*

"Blessed be he that enlargeth Gad: he dwelleth as a lion, and teareth the arm with the crown of the head.

And he provided the first

| BLESSINGS BY JACOB | BLESSINGS BY MOSES |
|---|---|
| | part for himself, because there, in a portion of the lawgiver, was he seated; and he came with the heads of the people, he executed the justice of the LORD, and his judgments with Israel." (Deut. 33:20-21.) |
| **ASHER,** *son of Leah's maid Zilpah* | **ASHER,** *son of Leah's maid Zilpah* |
| "Out of Asher his bread shall be fat, and he shall yield royal dainties." (Gen. 49:20.) | "Let Asher be blessed with children; let him be acceptable to his brethren, and let him dip his foot in oil. Thy shoes shall be iron and brass; and as thy days, so shall thy strength be." (Deut. 33:24-25.) |
| **NAPHTALI,** *son of Rachel's maid Bilhah* | **NAPHTALI,** *son of Rachel's maid Bilhah* |
| "Naphtali is a hind let loose: he giveth goodly words." (Gen. 49:21.) | "O Naphtali, satisfied with favour, and full with the blessing of the LORD: possess thou the west and the south." (Deut. 33:23.) |
| **JOSEPH,** *son of Rachel* | **JOSEPH,** *son of Rachel* |
| "Joseph is a fruitful bough, even a fruitful bough by a well; whose branches run over the wall: The archers have sorely grieved him, and shot at him, and hated him: But his bow abode in strength, and the arms of his | "Blessed of the Lord be his land, for the precious things of heaven, for the dew, and for the deep that coucheth beneath. And for the precious fruits brought forth by the sun, and for the precious things put forth by the moon, And for the chief things of |

## BLESSINGS BY JACOB

hands were made strong by the hands of the mighty God of Jacob; (from thence is the shepherd, the stone of Israel;)

Even by the God of thy father, who shall help thee; and by the Almighty, who shall bless thee with blessings of heaven above, blessings of the deep that lieth under, blessings of the breasts, and of the womb:

The blessings of thy father have prevailed above the blessings of my progenitors unto the utmost bound of the everlasting hills: they shall be on the head of Joseph, and on the crown of the head of him that was separate from his brethren." (Gen. 49:22-26.)

BENJAMIN, *son of Rachel*

"Benjamin shall ravin as a wolf: in the morning he shall devour the prey, and at night he shall divide the spoil." (Gen. 49:27.)

## BLESSINGS BY MOSES

the ancient mountains, and for the precious things of the lasting hills,

And for the precious things of the earth and fulness thereof, and for the good will of him that dwelt in the bush: let the blessing come upon the head of Joseph, and upon the top of the head of him that was separated from his brethren.

His glory is like the firstling of his bullock, and his horns are like the horns of unicorns: with them he shall push the people together to the ends of the earth: and they are the ten thousands of Ephraim, and they are the thousands of Manasseh." (Deut. 33:13-17.)

BENJAMIN, *son of Rachel*

"The beloved of the Lord shall dwell in safety by him; and the LORD shall cover him all the day long, and he shall dwell between his shoulders." (Deut. 22:12.)

# POSITION OF TRIBES WHEN CAMPING AND MARCHING IN THE WILDERNESS

### See Numbers 2

ON THE EAST THE
CAMP OF JUDAH
*first*
*verse 3, 9*

JUDAH
*verse 3*

ISSACHAR
*next to Judah*
*verse 5*

*then*
ZEBULUN
*verse 9*

⬆

EAST
Toward the
Promised Land

ON THE NORTH
THE CAMP OF DAN
*hindmost*
*verse 25, 31*

DAN
*verse 25*

ASHER
*by Dan*
*verse 27*

*then*
NAPHTALI
*verse 29*

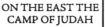

LEVI WITH THE
TABERNACLE
*in the midst*
*of the camp*
*verse 17*

ON THE SOUTH THE
CAMP OF REUBEN
*second rank*
*verse 10, 16*

REUBEN
*verse 10*

SIMEON
*by Reuben*
*verse 12*

*then*
GAD
*verse 14*

ON THE WEST THE
CAMP OF EPHRAIM
*third rank*
*verse 18, 24*

EPHRAIM
*verse 18*

MANASSEH
*by Ephraim*
*verse 20*

*then*
BENJAMIN
*verse 22*

# GATES OF FUTURE JERUSALEM
# TO BE NAMED FOR TRIBES

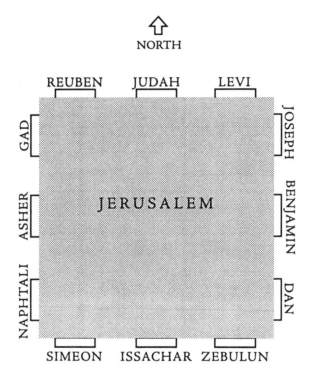

And the gates of the city shall be after the names of the tribes of Israel: three gates northward; one gate of Reuben, one gate of Judah, one gate of Levi.

And at the east side ... three gates; and one gate of Joseph, one gate of Benjamin, one gate of Dan.

And at the south side ... three gates; one gate of Simeon, one gate of Issachar, one gate of Zebulun.

At the west side ... three gates; one gate of Gad, one gate of Asher, one gate of Naphtali. (Ezekiel 48:31-34.)

# ADDITIONAL INFORMATION ON THE TRIBES

## THE RIFT BETWEEN JUDAH AND THE TEN TRIBES

When the northern tribes rebelled, forming two nations, the southern kingdom of Judah was mainly the tribes of Judah plus Benjamin which was absorbed. The northern kingdom of Israel was a ten-tribe nation, thus the collective name. This northern territory, however, was sometimes called the kingdom of Ephraim after the dominant tribe. In many respects the rift was an old rivalry between Judah, who was promised the sceptre, and Ephraim, who was given the birthright, each claiming the right to leadership.

Eventually, "The envy also of Ephraim shall depart, and the adversaries of Judah shall be cut off: Ephraim shall not envy Judah, and Judah shall not vex Ephraim." (Is. 11:13.)

## THE NAME OF THE TEN TRIBES

The Lord said through Isaiah, "Ye are they that forsake the LORD, that forget my holy mountain ... for the LORD GOD shall ... call his servants by another name." (Is. 65:11, 15.) The "holy mountain" stands for the laws and covenants given to the house of Israel through Moses. In other words, since the children of Israel did not want Him to be their God, He would not be their God and would remove His name from them. By this He meant the name El, so the name Isra-El was lost.

The next step, then, was this: "And thou shalt be called by a new name, which the mouth of the LORD shall name." (Is. 62:2.) So the Lord clearly said He would state the replacement name. He did so—"In Isaac shall thy seed by called." (Gen. 21:12; Rom. 9:7; Heb. 11:18.)

A respected historian of years ago commented, "The house of Judah never was called 'in Isaac,' but is called in Judah. The title Judah's sons evolved into the national name Jews. By a like evolution, 'Isaac's Sons' becomes Saxons as the new name applied to the house of Israel."[1] He backed up his statement with a speech by Brigham Young.

> *We are now gathering the children of Abraham who have come through the loins of Joseph and his sons, more especially through Ephraim, whose children are mixed among all the nations of the earth. The sons of Ephraim are wild and uncultivated, unruly, ungovernable. The spirit in them is turbulent and resolute; they are the Anglo-Saxon race, and they are upon the face of the whole earth.... I see a congregation of them before me today.*[2]

## IDENTIFYING THE TEN TRIBES

The historian suggested we "get fixed in our minds the one fact of Bible, Book of Mormon and Doctrine and Covenants, that the Ten Tribes were lost only as to their identity and not as to their location, which has always been given as the 'north countries' and the 'Isles of the sea.' The Lord has now begun to reveal their identity."[3]

"Whenever you find a people doing what Israel was to do, you have discovered the Identity."[4]

## CLUES TO LOCATIONS

"We hear of the maritime tribe of Israel, the tribe of Dan, whose ships are often mentioned in the Old Testament, and we find Dan's habit of leaving his name in all the places he visited, and we think it can be traced in the Rivers Danube and Dneiper and in Dardana and in Danmark and in Dannaans, the early inhabitants of Ireland."[5]

Other examples are the "Danaana of Ireland and the Danes of Denmark"[6]

In the Gaelic language, the name of the Irish Free State (1922-1937) is "Tuatha de Danaan. Translated into English it is Tribe of Dan."[7] Gaelic was used by the "Ga-els which means 'sons of God.'"[8]

"All the Scots are Gaels, and that name is a perfect derivative from Galilee, the home of Israel.... I find it again in the name of Gaul, for France.... And when I read in history that the French kings had Scottish regiments for their body guards, I do not wonder—they were both Gaels."[9] Galilee "included the territories of Issachar,

Naphtali, Zebulun, and Asher." (LDS Bible Dictionary, p. 677.) Dan bordered on the north.

# ANCIENT RECORDS

A former mission president of Mongolia mentioned that a lot of their records "were lost when the Russians came in. They didn't want family records." He didn't know what records there are, but "there are verbal records." (H.H.) According to ancient Mongolian lore, by about 150 years after the death of Christ there were 200,000 Christians in Mongolia. We can only speculate as to their records.

A sister from Armenia said, "Scriptures of Christ from 400 A.D. are in the Museum" of Ancient Manuscripts in the city of Yerevan. By this she meant that records much like the New Testament have been preserved since 400 A.D. She has been there and has seen them. She has a photograph of a manuscript of the Last Supper with a painting on the top half and the ancient words on the bottom half.

Another Armenian mentioned the museum has allowed the Church to microfilm all 15,000 ancient manuscripts, which included seven million names of genealogy.

These early religious records and genealogy, preserved for hundreds of years, are now in the hands of the Church. Our latter-day scripture says the tribes of Israel "shall bring forth their rich treasures unto the children of Ephraim." (D&C 133:30.) While we look forward to full fulfillment of this prophesy, surely already these are treasures.

## SOURCES

1. James H. Anderson, *God's Covenant Race*, Salt Lake City: Deseret News Press, 1938, p. 102.

2. *Ibid.*, quoting from *Discourses of Brigham Young*, p. 670.

3. *Ibid.*, p. 128.

4. *Ibid.*, p. 351.

5. *Ibid.*, p. 341.

6. *Ibid.*, p. 345.

7. *Ibid*, p. 48.

8. *Ibid.*, p. 345.

9. *Ibid.*, p. 342-343.

# SUGGESTED READING

"About Patriarchal Blessings," *New Era*, Mar. 2004, pp. 32-35.

Allred, Richard D., "The Lord Blesses His Children through Patriarchal Blessings," *Ensign*, Nov. 1997, pp. 27-28; "A Revelation for You," *New Era*, Nov. 1998, p. 46.

Beck, Julie B., "You Have a Noble Birthright," *Ensign*, May 2006, pp. 106-108.

Faust, James E., "Patriarchal Blessings," *New Era*, Nov. 1982, p. 4.

Faust, James E., "Priesthood Blessings," *Ensign*, Nov. 1995, pp. 62-64.

"Gaining Strength through Patriarchal Blessings," *Ensign*, June 1994, p. 53.

Lindsay, Richard P., "Chart Your Course by It," *New Era*, Sept. 1990. p. 4.

Millet, Robert L. and Joseph Fielding McConkie, *Our Destiny: the Call and Election of the House of Israel*, Salt Lake City: Bookcraft, 1993.

Monson, Thomas S., "Your Patriarchal Blessing: A Liahona of Light," *Ensign*, Nov. 1986. p. 65.

Packer, Boyd K., "The Stake Patriarch," *Ensign*, Nov. 2002, pp. 42-45.

Swanson, Vern G. "Israel's 'Other Tribes,'" *Ensign*, Jan. 1982, pp. 26-31.

"Teaching Children about Patriarchal Blessings," *Ensign*, Oct. 1987, p. 54.

Tvedtnes, John A. "The 'Other Tribes': Which Are They?" *Ensign*, Jan. 1982, pp. 31-32.

# APPENDIX II

| UNDERSTANDING YOUR BLESSING | | | |
|---|---|---|---|
| Mission or Central Idea: | | | |
| Blessings<br>*Things given* | Warnings<br>*Things to beware* | Counsel<br>*Things to do* | Promises<br>*Things conditional* |
|  |  |  |  |

+ Permission is given to copy and enlarge this page and the following page for personal and Church use.
+ Categories may be color-coded on an extra copy of your blessing.

# INFORMATION FOR FAMILY BLESSINGS

Name_____ Birth Date _____

Stake_____ No._____

Date _____ City_____ State _____

Patriarch giving blessing_____


Name_____ Birth Date _____

Stake_____ No._____

Date _____ City_____ State _____

Patriarch giving blessing_____


Name_____ Birth Date _____

Stake_____ No._____

Date _____ City_____ State _____

Patriarch giving blessing_____


Name_____ Birth Date _____

Stake_____ No._____

Date _____ City_____ State _____

Patriarch giving blessing_____

# Index

# ABOUT THE AUTHOR

**Gayla Stokes Wise** received her patriarchal blessing at age seventeen but never felt that she understood it or knew how to use it in her life. Believing others also had questions, this became the impetus for writing *The Power of Your Patriarchal Blessing.*

Sister Wise grew up in Idaho and Minnesota, a daughter of convert parents. She graduated from Utah State University with scholastic honors. Four days later she married the man she had met at age twelve. She has spent most of her life since then in Arizona.

Among her many callings, she has served as Young Women's president, Relief Society president, and Gospel Doctrine teacher. She taught teenagers in public schools before having children and for many years in the Church thereafter.

She and her husband Joseph B. Wise are the parents of five children and a growing number of grandchildren.